T0361171

Social Theory

First published in 1920, *Social Theory* endeavours to put together the social contents of various experiences of the ordinary man, and to make them, as far as they form one, a coherent and consistent whole. Social theory is not concerned directly with all the actions of individual men, but mainly with their actions taken in concert through some temporary or permanent organized group, and with the actions of such groups as they affect and react upon the individual. It is not primarily concerned with the State but with the whole problem of human association – that is, of associative will and action. This book will be of interest to students of economics, political science and sociology.

Social Theory

G. D. H. Cole

Routledge
Taylor & Francis Group

First published in 1920
By Methuen & Co. Ltd.

This edition first published in 2023 by Routledge
4 Park Square, Milton Park, Abingdon, Oxon, OX14 4RN
and by Routledge
605 Third Avenue, New York, NY 10017

Routledge is an imprint of the Taylor & Francis Group, an informa business

© Methuen & Co., 1920

Publisher's Note
The publisher has gone to great lengths to ensure the quality of this reprint but points out that some imperfections in the original copies may be apparent.

Disclaimer
The publisher has made every effort to trace copyright holders and welcomes correspondence from those they have been unable to contact.

A Library of Congress record exists under LCCN: 20006354

ISBN: 978-1-032-52187-9 (hbk)
ISBN: 978-1-003-40594-8 (ebk)
ISBN: 978-1-032-52285-2 (pbk)

Book DOI 10.4324/9781003405948

SOCIAL THEORY

BY

G. D. H. COLE

FELLOW OF MAGDALEN COLLEGE, OXFORD

AUTHOR OF

"SELF-GOVERNMENT IN INDUSTRY"
"LABOUR IN THE COMMONWEALTH" ETC.

METHUEN & CO. LTD.
36 ESSEX STREET W.C.
LONDON

First Published in 1920

CONTENTS

SOCIAL THEORY

CHAPTER I

THE FORMS OF SOCIAL THEORY.

M EN do not make communities—they are born and bred into them. Every individual at his birth is flung into a social environment, and his life's work from infancy is to make the best of that environment for himself and for his fellows. As he grows to fuller consciousness, his environment gradually expands. He becomes aware of the family, contact with which furnishes his first social experience. At the same time, he becomes aware also of a larger world outside the family, a world of wisdom, of things seen from windows and on journeys from home, a world which slowly assumes definite shapes and takes on human characteristics of neighbourhood and similarity. As he grows older, the fact of organisation in this world becomes apparent, and school, church, club and other social institutions claim him, and assume a part in his life. By the time he reaches manhood, he has drunk in and accepted the fact of the world, his environment, as a complex of individuals and associations, of customs and institutions, of rights and duties, of pleasures, pains, desires, hopes and fears, strivings and attempts to understand all centring round this complex and all raising the more or less insistent question of his place in it, and his relation to it.

Of course, this process is widely different in the case of different individuals, types and classes. Hitherto, men have usually been brought far sooner and more completely into contact with an organised social environment than women, whose experience has not been allowed to expand with the same freedom. Again, the opportunities of the rich and of the educated classes for contact with the world without have been far fuller than those of the workers or of the lower middle class. The workers, however, through their Trade Unions, clubs and other societies have shared with the upper classes what is largely denied to the lower middle class — the opportunity for free association with a communal object, and the consequent appreciation of the social structure of the world around them. The Trade Union is the working-class equivalent for the upper-class public school and university, which are the scenes not so much of education, as of the social training of a ruling caste.

The generality of men and women take their experience of the social scene around them unphilosophically. They do not reflect upon it ; they merely accept it. But that does not make it any the less a real experience, or any the less a part of their mental equipment. They are born into a complex society, and by a natural process that complex society becomes a part of their lives—as

THE FORMS OF SOCIAL THEORY

real a *Weltanschauung* as any Teutonic philosopher ever imagined.

The task which I propose to attempt in this book is that of setting down, as clearly as I can, the social content of this *Weltanschauung* of the ordinary man, not of course limiting myself to what he sees, but endeavouring to put together the social contents of various experiences, and to make of them, as far as they form one, a coherent and consistent whole. What is the content of our social experience—what is the relation between the various fragmentary experiences and contacts of and with individuals, associations and institutions which we come upon in our day-to-day life in Society? What, in short, is the structure of the half-organised and half-conscious community of which we form a part?

Perhaps that last question gives rather too large and inclusive an idea of the purpose which I have in mind. It is not *all* experience that I mean to deal with, but only social experience. Social Theory is not concerned directly with all the actions of individual men, but mainly with their actions taken in concert through some temporary or permanent organised group, and with the actions of such groups as they affect and react upon the individual. The unorganised, personal conduct of individual men will be always present as the background of our study, though it will only be treated incidentally in relation to its social content.

Even with this limitation, the scope which I have taken for this book will seem to many people far too wide. Social Theory, especially under its name of ' Political Theory,' has often been regarded as

3

having to do mainly with one particular association, the State, and with its relation to the individual. Recent theory, however, has been moving more and more to the conclusion that this definition of the scope of the subject is wrong, because it is fundamentally untrue to the facts of social experience.

I do not mean, of course, to deny that it is possible to write books about, and even to make a distinct and separate study of, the nature of the association called ' The State,' and its relation to the individual. That is, of course, a perfectly legitimate and necessary inquiry. But I do absolutely deny that any study of the relations of State and individual can furnish even the groundwork for a general survey of social experience, and that it, taken by itself, can penetrate to the heart of the question of man's place in Society. It is simply not true that the social relations of which a man is most directly and constantly aware are, under normal conditions, his relations with the State ; and it is still less true that these relations furnish the whole, or even the greater part, of his social experience.

Society is a very complex thing. Apart from personal and family relations, almost every individual in it has, from childhood onwards, close contacts with many diverse forms of social institution and association. Not only is he a citizen or subject of his State, and of various local governing authorities within it : he is also related to the social order through many other voluntary or involuntary associations and institutions. He is, maybe, a worker in a factory, mine or office, a member of a

church or other religious or irreligious body, a
Trade Unionist or member of a professional or
trading association, a Co-operator or Allotment
Holder or Building or Friendly Society member, he
has his club of the Pall Mall, political or workman's
variety, he is a sportsman associated with his
fellow-sportsman, a Socialist or a Primrose Leaguer,
he has hobbies which cause him to join an association
of persons with the same tastes, or views which
cause him to link up with others of the same opinion.
Moreover, as a husband and a house or share owner,
he is directly in contact with the social institutions
of marriage and property, while his whole life is a
complex in which social customs and traditions play
an immense part. None can escape from constant
contact with some of these various social relations,
and almost every one is conscious of a widely diversified and ceaselessly varying social environment of
which he forms, for his fellows, a part. Custom is
perhaps strongest among women, and association
is certainly strongest among men ; but among women
also the growth of association is following hard upon
the awakening of a wider social consciousness.

This being the character of the social complex,
the question at once arises of the right way of
surveying it from the theoretic standpoint. The
tendency of political theorists has been to survey it
under the guidance of the principle of Power or
Force, which is also the principle of the Austinian
theory of law. Of all the forms of association and
institution which I have mentioned, only the State,
and, under the State, in a small degree the local
authority, obviously possesses in our day coercive

power. The State, therefore, as the ' determinate superior,' having in its hands not only the majesty of law, but the ultimate weapon of physical compulsion, has been singled out and set on a pedestal apart from all other forms of association, and treated as *the* social institution *par excellence*, beside which all other associations are merely corporate or quasi-corporate individuals, which the State and the law can only recognise at all by pretending that they are individuals, although it is perfectly plain that they are not.

Following out this line of thought to its logical conclusion, classical Political Theory has treated the State as the embodiment and representative of the social consciousness, the State's actions as the actions of men in Society, the relations of the State and the individual as the chief, and almost the only, subject-matter of Social Theory. Over against the State and its actions and activities this form of theory has set indiscriminately the whole complex of individuals and other associations and institutions, and has treated all their manifestations as individual actions without vital distinction or difference.

I believe that this false conception of the subject arises mainly from the conception of human society in terms of Force and Law. It begins at the wrong end, with the coercion which is applied to men in Society, and not with the motives which hold men together in association. The other way of conceiving human Society, first fully developed in Rousseau's *Social Contract*, is in terms not of Force or Law, but of Will.

As soon as we view the social scene in this light,

6

the whole outlook is at once different. Not only the State, but all the other forms of association in which men join or are joined together for the execution of any social purpose, are seen as expressing and embodying in various manners and degrees the wills of the individuals who compose them. The distinction between Social Theory—the theory of social conduct—and Ethics—the theory of individual conduct—is at once seen to be the distinction between simple individual action and associative action, between the direct individual action of a human being by the simple translation of his will into deed, and the associative action of a number of human beings, or of an individual acting on behalf of a number as agent or representative, through a society or association. Of course, the act of an individual may be just as ' social ' in its content and purpose as the act of a society or group. But that is not the point : the vital point is that, viewed in terms of will, the actions of the State appear as of the same nature with the actions of any other association in which men are joined together for a common purpose. The respective spheres of ethical and social theory are thus marked out with sufficient clearness for practical purposes, though a doubtful borderland remains of types of action which can be regarded as either personal or associative, because the element of association, though present in them, is present in so rudimentary a form as not to override the purely individual element. This point, however, does not concern us here ; for it is enough for the present to have made it clear that Social Theory is concerned primarily, not with the State, but with the whole problem of human association—that is, of associative will and action.

It is, of course, possible to reject will as the basis of human institutions; but the consequences of such a rejection are so extraordinary that nearly all political theorists have recoiled from their direct acceptance. Even those who, like Hobbes, have been most assiduous in founding their conception of actual societies on the basis of Force and Law, have sought to reinforce their position by finding an original basis for social association in will. Hence Hobbes' imaginary original social contract in which men bound themselves together by Will into a society, only to alienate for ever for themselves and their posterity the will which alone could make their society legitimate. As soon as a basis of right, and not of mere fact, is sought for human association, there is no escape from invoking the principle of human will, except for those who maintain that Kings are Kings for ever by Divine Right and Appointment. And even this is only to appeal from the Will of man to an omnipresent and omnipotent Will of God.

Every approach to democracy makes the actual and legitimate foundation of Society on the will of its members more manifest. A theory based on Force and Law may pass for long undetected in an authoritarian Society; but it cannot survive the emergence of democratic or even of aristocratic consciousness. This is true, not only or mainly because the will of the people or of a class begins to exert its influence upon affairs of State; but, still more, because, without the sanction of law, other forms of democratic or oligarchal association begin to exercise a power which, within their sphere of operation, threatens to challenge or control the State and to usurp the functions which it has arrogated to itself. Law in the strict sense, law enforceable by courts and police, may remain in the hands of the State ; but other bodies, such as a baronial assembly, a Church or a Trade Union, frame regulations and secure their observance, even without the aid of the black cap and the policeman. To the great scandal of authority in our own day, even the policemen form a Trade Union of their own, and aim at becoming, within a narrow sphere, their own legislature, executive, and judiciary.

Such a social situation is fatal to Political Theory of the old type. While the political philosophers are holding high argument about the philosophical theory of the State, and the relation to it of the individual, the world around them has become interested in a new set of problems, in the position of voluntary and functional associations in Society, in their relation to national States, and their position as being often international associations, in the multiplicity and possible conflict of loyalties and obligations involved for the individual in simultaneous membership of several such associations. In short, while the philosophers are still arguing about the State and the individual, the world of creative thought has moved on to the discussion of the functional organisation of Society, and the new problems for the individual to which it gives rise.

AN INTRODUCTION TO SOCIAL THEORY

It is not in the least surprising that, under these conditions, the political theory of the schools has become sterile, and that the new developments have arisen among those whose vital interest has lain neither in philosophy nor in the State, but in the sphere of functional association. Apart from purely psychological developments, there are at present only three live sources of social theory—the Church, industry and history. Socially inarticulate in this country since the enfeebling conflicts of the seventeenth century, the Churches are to-day regaining their voice, if not their hold, upon the people. They are beginning to realise that they, too, are social institutions, and to reclaim their right to spiritual self-government and spiritual freedom from the State. Dr. J. N. Figgis's book, *Churches in the Modern State*, has proved itself one of the live forces in present-day social theory.

A force far more generally diffused, and far more potent in its influence, is that which springs from industrial sources. Bolsheviks, Syndicalists, Marxian Industrialists and Communists not merely claim for proletarian organisations independence of the State ; they threaten to destroy it altogether. Right or wrong, they are a force, and their doctrines are a living international influence. At the same time Guild Socialists, inspired also by industrial and economic conditions, preach the doctrine of democratic self-government in industry, and the transformation of the State by the influence of the functional principle. Their doctrine is far wider than industry, although it springs out of industrial conditions. It amounts in the last analysis to a

THE FORMS OF SOCIAL THEORY

complete Social Theory—to the Social Theory which I am putting forward in this book.

Thirdly, there is the source of history, which, as our knowledge of the past grows, reminds us more and more that the factotum State—the omnicompetent, omnivorous, omniscient, omnipresent Sovereign State—in so far as it exists at all outside the brain of megalomaniacs, is a thing of yesterday, and that functional association, which is now growing painfully to a fuller stature, is not a young upstart of our days, but has a pedigree to the full as long and as honourable as that of the State itself—and indeed longer and more honourable. Not only the study of mediæval history, but still more the growing knowledge of early human institutions, serves to emphasise the common character of the various forms of human association, the essential reality, based on the common will of men, of associations to which Roman law was prepared to concede only the derivative character of *personæ fictæ*. We owe much to Gierke and Maitland in the study of law; for they have enabled us to view it, not as the handmaid of the Sovereign State, but in its relation to human association as a whole.

Our study of Social Theory will begin, then, not with the State, or with any other particular form of association, but with association as a whole, and the way in which men act through associations in supplement and complement to their actions as isolated or private individuals.

Here, however, we are confronted with an immediate difficulty. Is the family to be treated as an association, and therefore as part of the social

11

fabric of Society as distinguished from the individuals composing it ? Does the study of the family form a part of the study of individual conduct or of social conduct ? These are not easy questions to answer.

I do not propose to go deeply into the historical character of the family, or to touch at all upon the relations, actual or supposed, between the family and the tribe. I am treating my subject, not historically, but purely in relation to the present and the future. I shall therefore say only that, in modern times, the family has changed not only its nature and function, but also its composition, and that in doing so it has become far less a social and far more a purely personal unit. The family to-day only functions as a unit in relation to the personal concerns of a relatively very small group, usually those who are included in a single household or brick-box. The family, in the sense of the clan, including a large group of blood kindred, no longer survives in Western Countries as a social unit. It was, in primitive civilisation, distinctly and markedly a social rather than a personal unit ; but to-day the social functions of the clan have passed into other hands, and the family remains as a private group largely bereft of social functions except in the getting and upbringing of children. No small exception, truly ! But it is an exception largely irrelevant to our present purposes. For, although in a sense the family is the necessary basis of Society, it remains itself, under modern conditions, largely external to the social fabric, the scene of purely personal contacts and least capable of organisation where it is most performing a social function. Its very character is to be unorganisable, incapable of organised co-ordination with the world of associations which surrounds it ; in short, personal rather than collective, individual rather than associative in its operation. It is itself perhaps the strongest of all human groups, as it is certainly the most permanent ; but, as a human group, it is essentially individual, and not the least of its strength lies in the fact that it holds aloof from other groups and remains, to a great extent, isolated in a world of developing interrelation. Its members exercise their civic, industrial and political functions more and more, not through it, but as individuals, and, by the removal of other past functions, the disappearance of domestic industry for instance, it is more and more set free to become the sphere of purely personal affections and contacts.

In the past, some social theorists have based their whole theory upon the analogy of the family, and have striven to explain all wider phenomena of association and community in its light.[1] Any such explanation seems to-day so obviously misleading that it need not detain us at all. It is, however, important to point out that this is by no means the only cure in which the use of a false analogy has caused social theories to suffer shipwreck. Again and again, social theorists, instead of finding and steadily employing a method and a terminology proper to their subject, have attempted to express the facts and values of Society in terms of some other theory or science. On the analogy of the

[1] *e.g.* Filmer's *Patriarcha.*

13

physical sciences they have striven to analyse and explain Society as *mechanism*, on the analogy of biology they have insisted on regarding it as an *organism*, on the analogy of mental science or philosophy they have persisted in treating it as a *person*, sometimes on the religious analogy they have come near to confusing it with a God.

These various analogies have very different degrees of value and disvalue. The mechanical analogy and the organic analogy have been alike definitely harmful, and have led theory seriously astray ; for they both invoke a material analogy in what is essentially a mental or spiritual study. The analogies drawn from psychology and mental philosophy are far less harmful, and may be even extremely suggestive, if they are not pushed too far ; for though neither Society nor the various associations which it includes are ' persons,' they approach far more nearly to being persons than to being either mechanical or organic.

There are, however, obvious and sufficient reasons why no analogy can carry the study of human Society very far forward. To every distinct human study corresponds its own method and its own terminology, and analogy pushed beyond very restricted limits necessarily engenders confusion. Our object is not to know what Society is like, but to know what and how it is ; and any reference of it to some other body of knowledge defeats the object in view.

It is true that the method of social theory bears a close resemblance to the method of ethics and psychology. The two are, indeed, in a very real sense, complementary, and only in both groups of knowledge together can we find a full knowledge of community. They must pursue to a great extent the same method, in order to arrive at conclusions which are capable of being collated and correlated. Thus social theory has its social psychology, its descriptive study of the action of men in association, and this is related to social philosophy to some extent, though not wholly in the same way as individual psychology is related to moral philosophy.[1] How far the parallel holds depends largely upon the sphere assigned to social psychology, which is a young science not yet at all sure of its scope or method.

The fact, however, that social and moral theory are complementary, and that, as the final object of both is the human mind in action, they must pursue largely and essentially the same method, is only one reason the more for keeping their terminologies as clearly distinct as possible. For their spheres of operation are distinct, though closely related, and the closeness of their relationship only makes any confusion of terminology the more likely to result in confusion of thought. Thus, if we say that an association is a ' person,' we are merely obscuring a difference—between persons and associations, or rather between personal and associative action, upon which the separate existence of moral and social theory essentially depends. Such a conception may be useful to lawyers whose object is to be able to group persons and associations together for like treatment civilly under the law ; but it is clearly inadmissible in social theory.

[1] To this point I must return later. See p. 18.

We must, then, avoid analogies, or at the least avoid allowing our terminology to be influenced at all by analogies, however valuable. We must adopt our own terminology, and make it, as far as possible, clearly distinct from the terminology of any other study.

So far, I am fully aware, the ground has not been cleared for the adoption of an easily intelligible and consistent terminology for social theory. This is in part, but only in part, the fault of social theorists, who have not succeeded in defining with sufficient exactitude the scope and the boundaries of their inquiry. It must, however, be recognised that the task is one of peculiar difficulty, both because the words of social theory are words of common use and wont, and therefore peculiarly liable to shift their meaning as conditions change, and still more because conditions do change, and the associations and institutions with which social theory has to deal change with them, develop new functions, and discard old ones, and even alter their fundamental character and internal structure. The ' States ' of to-day differ widely among themselves, and we should be hard put to it to find a definition which would embrace them all. But the ' States ' of different ages differ far more widely, until such common nature as exists among them is almost undiscernible in the mass of transient characteristics which encompass them at every time.

If, then, this book seems to be concerned largely with questions of terminology, that is not my fault. It is hardly possible to fall into any discussion upon an important point of social theory without finding sooner or later the discussion tending to resolve itself into a question of words—not because only words are at issue, but because it is impossible to get down to the real issues until verbal ambiguities have been removed. We shall be unable to proceed with any analysis of social phenomena, and still more with any explanation of them, until we have determined, as far as possible, to use each important name only in a single and definite sense, and until we have agreed what that definite sense is to be. That is why my second chapter deals entirely with questions of terminology.

Before, however, we begin the discussion of these vexed questions, it will be well to make as plain as possible the object which this book has in view. The subject-matter of social theory is the action of men in association. That is clear enough. But manifestly this subject-matter can be studied from several different points of view. Apart from purely historical studies, there are at least three main ways—besides many subsidiary ways—of approaching it, and, while each of the resulting bodies of knowledge is useful to each of the others, and each throws a necessary light upon each, their respective interests are clearly distinct and the generalisations or results with which they are concerned are essentially different. We must see clearly what is the content of these various studies, if we are to recognise and appreciate the scope and the limitations of that study with which alone we are here directly concerned.

The first way of approach to social theory lies through the study and comparison of actual social institutions. Here it often approaches nearly to history ; for the direct material with which it works is to be found in history. The anthropologist or sociologist, studying the institutions of primitive mankind, the constitutional historian, studying the evolution of the State and of the political structure of Society, the jurist, studying the development of law, the ecclesiastical historian, studying the growth and organisation of churches—all these amass materials from which generalisations can be drawn, and on which more or less scientific principles of human organisation can be based. The student of representative institutions—a Montesquieu or an Ostrogorski—works upon these materials and arrives at results which possess an objective value. A ' positive science ' of institutions is the object of such forms of inquiry.

The second way of approach lies through the study, not of institutions in themselves, but of the motives and impulses by which men are moved in their social actions through institutions and associations. At one extreme, this type of theory finds its place in the study of ' mob ' or ' crowd ' psychology, the impulses and ways of action of a barely organised human group. At the other extreme, it studies, from the same standpoint, the psychological aspects of the most complicated and highly developed form of social association, and endeavours, like the psychology of individual conduct, to formulate the general rules which guide the actions of men in association, studying also the diseases of association as individual psychology studies the diseases of personality. Mr. Robert Michels's book on *Demo-*

THE FORMS OF SOCIAL THEORY

cracy and the Organisation of Political Parties is perhaps the best modern example of this form of study in its developed form ; but the nucleus of it is to be found in that part of Rousseau's *Social Contract* which deals with the actions of ' government,' and the tendency of all governments to degenerate.[1]

There is, of course, much ' Social Psychology ' which takes for itself a far more roving commission than this. Like psychology as a whole, Social Psychology has often tended, in the hands of its professors, to rely too much on data afforded by the primitive types, and to resolve itself largely into an analysis of instincts. Mr. Graham Wallas's *Human Nature in Politics* furnished a sort of preface to a more developed sort of Social Psychology, which its author proceeded to follow up, somewhat disappointingly, in *The Great Society*. In America, however, the method of Mr. Wallas is finding followers in plenty, and big developments of this form of social study may be expected from these sources.

The third way of approach to social theory is that which Rousseau explicitly set out to attempt in the first two books of his *Social Contract*. It is no less than the discovery of universal principles of social association—of the values, rather than of the facts—of sociality. He contrasted his own method sharply with that of Montesquieu in the following passage :—

" Montesquieu did not intend to treat of the principles of political right ; he was content to

[1] See *Social Contract*, bk. iii., especially chap. x.

treat of the positive law of established governments ; and no two studies could be more different than these." [1]

Thus, in Rousseau's view, the way of approach which he sought to adopt in discovering the philosophic principles of human association was a way which concerned itself not with fact, but with *right*. It was, in the language of the schools, a *normative*, and not a positive study. It was thus complementary and parallel to ethical philosophy as the study of individual conduct from the moral standpoint, just as social psychology, the study of associative conduct from the descriptive, analytical and comparative point of view, corresponds to individual psychology, as the study of individual conduct from the same point of view. Here, however, the parallel breaks down because of the difference of subject-matter. In the case of social institutions, there is a third way of study—the first of those mentioned above—which examines and compares actual institutions and endeavours to reach practical generalisations on this basis. In the case of individual conduct, there is no corresponding third way, unless we consent to regard the study of the human body—physiological psychology, physiology proper, and all the other sciences which have to do with the body—as in some sense parallel. But to do this is to fall into one of those dangerous analogies against which we have already uttered a warning. Actual institutions may be likened, in a certain sense, to the ' body ' of the community, as they may be

[1] *Emile*, bk. v. The word *droit* in the French is used in the sense both of ' right ' (*droit politique*) and ' law ' (*droit positif*).

regarded as, in a certain sense, its mechanism. But strictly speaking, the community has no body and, as Herbert Spencer said, no ' common sensorium.' Institutions, even if we abstract from the motives which are present in their action, are neither organism nor mechanism. We may, if we will, speak of the " organs of the body social," or of the " machinery of Society," but we must beware of regarding such phrases as more than metaphors, or of basing any conclusions at all upon them.

My object in this book is primarily philosophical. I am concerned principally with social theory as the social complement of ethics, with ' ought ' rather than with ' is,' with questions of right rather than of fact. But this does not mean that it is desirable or possible to extrude from consideration the other forms of social study which have been mentioned. Social psychology of the type described above offers, in particular, indispensable material for any study of social conduct. The difference is that, in relation to the particular inquiry upon which we are setting out, it forms part, not of the ultimate interest or object before us, but of the material on which we have to work. We must know how associations and institutions actually work, what human motives and distortions of human motive are actually present in them, before we can form any philosophical conception of the principles on which they rest. We therefore cannot quite say, like Rousseau, " Away with all the facts ! " although in our conclusions the facts drop away and only questions of right remain.

There is a further danger, not yet directly mentioned, against which we must be, throughout the study, always on our guard. It is the more necessary to guard against it, because the essential difficulties of terminology are always drawing us into it, whether we will or not. We must avoid thinking of either the State or the community as ends in themselves, as self-subsistent and individual realities similar to, or greater than, the persons who are members of them. We must never say that the State desires this, or the community wills that, or the Church is aiming at so and so, without realising clearly that the only wills that really exist are the wills of the individual human beings who have become members of these bodies. There is no such thing, strictly speaking, as the ' will ' of an association or institution; there are only the co-operating wills of its members.

The chief difficulty here arises from two sources. First, from the fact that the actions of an association seldom if ever reflect the wills of all its members—there is practically always a dissentient minority, and very often an apathetic majority. Secondly, from the fact that an association often seems to acquire a sort of momentum which impels it into action without the force of any individual will behind it, or at least causes big actions to be taken on a very small and weak basis of will. Both these facts easily lead us to ascribe a will to the institution itself—a will in some sense transcending the wills of its members. Burke's *French Revolution* arrives at this position by the second route ; Bosanquet's *Philosophical Theory of the State* and much other more or less Hegelian writing by the first. Rousseau sometimes seems to fall into the same error, though his way of arriving at it is more obscure.

This is a question which will have to be discussed much more fully later in this book. Here it need only be said that, even if the belief underlying the view of State or community or association as an ' end in itself ' were true, it would be none the less important to keep our ways of speaking about such ' ends in themselves ' clearly distinct from our ways of speaking about individual human beings. Otherwise, only serious confusion can result. Thus, if, like Rousseau, we use the term ' General Will ' to mean sometimes a will generally diffused among the citizens, and at other times to mean a will whose object is the general good of the citizens, whether it is present in the mind of one or some or all of them, the way is already paved to an illusory reconciliation of these two different meanings of terming this " General Will," which begins in either case as somebody's (or everybody's) will, into a will which is neither somebody's nor everybody's, but the will of the State or the community itself.

I have spoken so much of terminological difficulties and confusions that I fear the reader is already looking forward to the next chapter, which deals entirely with the use of terms, with considerable misgivings. But I hope I have said enough to make it plain that there is no chance of carrying this inquiry satisfactorily through to the end unless we begin by getting as clear as we can the sense in which the names on which it hinges are to be used. We cannot hope to get them quite clear, even to our own minds ; and still less can we hope to find any way of reconciling or making easily comparable the varying terminologies of different writers on our subject. But we must do the best we can, and crave indulgence if our definitions are not fully satisfactory.

To that task of clearing the ground for our main inquiry we must now turn.

CHAPTER II

SOME NAMES AND THEIR MEANING

E VERY developed *Community* may be regarded as giving rise to an organised *Society*, within which there exists a vast complex of social *customs, institutions* and *associations*, through which the *members* or citizens express themselves and secure in part the fulfilment of the various *purposes* which some or all of them have in common. There are in this sentence at least seven words upon the clear definition of which success in our subsequent inquiry largely depends.

Community is the broadest and most inclusive of the words which we have to define. By a ' Community ' I mean a complex of social life, a complex including a number of human beings living together under conditions of social relationship, bound together by a common, however constantly changing, stock of conventions, customs and traditions, and conscious to some extent of common social objects and interests. It will be seen at once that this is a very wide and elastic form of definition, under which a wide variety of social groups might be included. It is, indeed, of the essence of community that its definition should be thus elastic ; for ' community ' is essentially a subjective term, and the reality of it consists in the consciousness of it among its members. Thus a family is, or may be, a community, and any group which is, in a certain degree, self-contained and self-subsistent, is or may be a community. A mediæval University, a monastic brotherhood, a co-operative colony—these and many more may possess those elements of social comprehensiveness which give a right to the title of community.

But, if the word is wide and inclusive enough in one aspect, it is essentially limiting in another. In order to be a community, a group must exist for the good life and not merely for the furtherance of some specific and partial purpose. Thus, a cricket club, or a Trade Union, or a political party is not a community, because it is not a self-contained group of complete human beings, but an association formed for the furtherance of a particular interest common to a number of persons who have other interests outside it. A community is thus essentially a social unit or group to which human beings belong, as distinguished from an association with which they are only connected.

Yet, despite this wholeness and universality which are of the nature of community, it is not the case that a man can belong to one community only. A community is an inclusive circle of social life; but round many narrow circles of family may be drawn the wider circle of the city, and round many circles of city the yet wider circle of the Province or the Nation, while round all the circles of Nation is drawn the yet wider and more cosmopolitan circle of World civilisation itself. No one of these wider

NAMES AND THEIR MEANING

circles necessarily absorbs the narrower circles
within it : they may maintain themselves as real
and inclusive centres of social life within the wider
communities beyond them. A man is not less a
member of his family or a citizen of his city for being
an Englishman or a cosmopolitan. Membership of
two communities may lead, for the individual, to a
real conflict of loyalties ; but the reality of the
conflict only serves to measure the reality of the
communal obligation involved.

Our definition does not, of course, enable us to
say exactly and in every instance what is a community and what is not. Being a community is a
matter of degree, and all communities, being actual,
are also necessarily imperfect and incomplete.
There may often arise, not merely a dispute, but an
actual doubt in the minds of the persons concerned
to what community they belong, as for instance in
a border country which hardly knows with which of
the peoples it lies between its community of tradition, interest and feeling is the stronger. Again, a
province or a town may be merely an administrative
area, with no common life or feeling of its own, or it
may be a real and inclusive centre of social life.
Moreover, it may pass by insensible stages from the
one condition to the other, as when a depopulated
strip of countryside becomes first a formless urban
district and then gradually assumes the form and
feeling of a town or city, changes and developments
in administrative organisation usually, but not
necessarily, accompanying the change in feeling.
There are groups which obviously deserve the name
of communities, and groups which obviously do not

deserve it ; but there are also countless groups of which it is difficult to say, at any particular moment, whether they deserve the name or not.

It is plain, then, that our thing, ' a community,' does not necessarily involve any particular form of social organisation, or indeed any social organisation at all. It is not an institution or a formal association, but a centre of feeling, a group felt by its members to be a real and operative unity. In any community larger than the family, however, this feeling of unity, with its accompanying need for common action, almost necessarily involves conscious and formal organisation. The feeling of unity makes it easy for the members of a community to associate themselves together for the various purposes which they have in common, and, where the community is free from external hindrances, such association surely arises and is devoted to the execution of these common purposes. Where a community is not free, and an external power hinders or attempts to prevent organisation, association still asserts itself, but instead of directing itself to the fulfilment of the various social needs of the group, almost every association is diverted to subserve the task of emancipating the community from external hindrances. This, for instance, is the position in Ireland at the present time.

We are concerned in this study with community as a whole, and with communities of every kind ; but our chief interest is necessarily with those larger and more complex communities which have the largest social content and the most diversified social organisation. It is, indeed, in relation to these that the principal difficulties arise. The simple fact of community is easy enough to appreciate ; but in a large and highly developed social group, internal organisation, and cross-currents of organisation which, assignable to wider communities, overleap the frontiers of the smaller groups and communities within them, often loom so large that the fact of community itself tends to disappear from sight. The desire to counter this tendency is, as we shall see later, one of the principal causes of the facile, but fatal, identification of community with ' State ' which is so often made by social theorists.

"Every developed community," we began by declaring, "may be regarded as giving rise to an organised *Society*." In the small community of the family this distinction does not to-day, or usually, arise.[1] But for larger communities the distinction is of vital importance. In every such community there is a part of the common life which is definitely and formally organised, regulated by laws and directed by associations formed for social purposes. I mean to use the term *Society* to denote the complex of organised associations and institutions within the community.

I am conscious in this use of giving to the word ' Society ' a more definite meaning than those with which it is customarily employed. Indeed, the meaning here assigned to it is to a certain extent artificial, but by no means entirely so. We do in

---

[1] It does arise, wherever, as in tribal communities, the family becomes a centre of organised law-giving or justice, or directs the economic life of its members on a wide enough basis to require formal organisation.

fact constantly speak of Society when we wish to denote neither the whole complex of community, nor any particular association or institution, but the sum total of organised social structure which is the resultant of the various associations and institutions within a community. A word is necessary for our purposes to express our sense of that part of the common life which is organised, and the word ' Society ' seems the best fitted for this purpose.

' Society,' then, in the sense in which the word is used in this book, is not a complete circle of social life, or a social group of human beings, but a resultant of the interaction and complementary character of the various functional associations and institutions. Its concern is solely with the organised co-operation of human beings, and its development consists not directly in the feeling of community among individuals, but in the better coherence and more harmonious relationship of the various functional bodies within the community.

We have seen that a developed community, larger than the family, can hardly exist without institutions and associations ; that is, without Society. Society, on the other hand, may exist, if imperfectly, yet in a developed form, without real community, or with only a very slender basis of community. The union of Ireland and Great Britain under a single Parliament, and with a large system of associations and institutions extending to both, is an instance of a Society with but the shadow of a basis of community. In such a case, as we shall see, the more artificial an association or institution is, or the greater the element of coercion it includes, the more it is inclined to persist, whereas the more voluntary and spontaneous forms of organisation find it hard to live under such conditions. The growth of a purely Irish Labour Movement, with a tendency to break away from the British Movement, is an example of this difficulty.

Society, as a complex of organisations, cannot stand for, or express, all human life within a community, or the whole life of any single human being. Indeed, it is probably true that what is best and most human in men and women escapes almost entirely from the net of Society, because it is incapable of being organised. Society is concerned mainly with rights and duties, with deliberate purposes and interests. While the community is essentially a centre of feeling, Society is a centre, or rather a group of centres, of deliberation and planning, concerned far more with means than with ends. It is, of course, true that an association or an institution can arouse in us and make us attach to it sentiments of loyalty as well as calculated adherences ; but at least the better part of our feelings of love and devotion are put forth in purely personal relationships, or in the narrow but intense community of the family. It is essential that associations and institutions, and even that Society itself, should be able to appeal to our sentiments of loyalty and devotion, but it would be wrong to desire that these sentiments should be absorbed in them. As long as human life remains, most of the best things in it will remain outside the bounds and scope of organisation, and it will be the chief function of Society so to organise these parts of human life which respond to organisation as to afford the fullest opportunity for the development of those human experiences and relationships to which organisation is the cold touch of death.

Society, like community, is a matter of degree. It depends not only on the volume and extent of associative and institutional life in the community, but still more on the coherence and co-operative working of the various associations and institutions. Where associative and institutional life is vigorous, but there exist distinct castes and classes, each with its own network of organisations, not co-operating but conflicting and hostile, then Society exists indeed, but only in a very low degree. The highest development of Society consists not only in the general diffusion of associations and institutions over every organisable tract of social life, but also in the harmonious co-operation of all the various bodies, each fulfilling its proper function within Society, in harmony and agreement with the others. We shall be able to appreciate the full implications of this harmony better at a later stage, when we have examined more closely the nature of associations and institutions, and when we have shown in its true light the principle of ' function ' as their sustaining principle.

We have so far spoken of *associations* and *institutions* uncritically, without any attempt to examine their nature, or to define the sense in which the terms are used. To do this is our next task. We have seen that every developed community includes a network of associations and institutions of the most various kinds, and we have now to explain their character as far as we can. This is the central difficulty of our subject, and, if this is surmounted, we may fairly hope that much of the rest will be comparatively plain sailing.

Men living together in community are conscious of numerous wants, both material and spiritual. In order to satisfy these wants, they must take action, and accordingly they translate their consciousness of wants into will. These wants are of the most diverse character, and require the most diverse means for their satisfaction. In two respects above all, they differ fundamentally one from another, and their differences in these respects present the best starting-point for our examination.

Some wants are of a simple character and only require a simple translation into will and action for their fulfilment, or for the demonstration that they cannot be fulfilled. Such wants, being essentially simple and single, do not give rise to any form of organisation. But very many wants are complex, and require for their fulfilment not a single act of will or action, but a whole course of action sustained by a continuing purpose. It is in such cases, where the will must be maintained over a whole course of action, that the need for organisation may arise.

The presence of deliberate purpose, however, does not necessarily lead to social organisation. The individual has often to present to himself a course of action, and to sustain by a continuing act of will a whole course of action. In such a case he may be said to ' organise ' his own mind, but organisation remains purely personal and within his mind. The position is different when he finds that the purpose before him can only, or can better, be furthered by his acting in common with other individuals and undertaking in common with them a course of action which, he hopes, will lead to the satisfaction of the want of which he is conscious in himself. The mere realisation of the need for co-operative action does not, of course, call the co-operation into being, but it is the basis on which co-operation can be built. This consciousness of a want requiring co-operative action for its satisfaction is the basis of *association*.

The wants which may lead to association are themselves of the most diverse kind, and can be classified in the most varied ways. The classification that is necessary for our present purpose is, however, clear enough. It is not the ' material,' but the ' social ' content of the want with which we are here concerned. In this aspect, the want may be either ' several ' or ' associative.' It is, of course, in either case a want of an individual, because only individuals *can* want anything ; but its nature may be such that each individual can enjoy the satisfaction of it by himself, even if imperfectly, whether the other individual secures a like satisfaction or not (these are the wants which I have here called ' several '), or it may be such that it can be enjoyed only by the co-operating group as a whole, and not by any individual except in conjunction with other individuals. Of course, if a want is complex in character, and is rather a circle of wants than a single want, it may partake of both natures, and be at once several and associative.

Both several and associative wants are fertile of

associations ; but the permanence and social value of the associations which they create differ considerably. A mere similarity or coincidence of object, while it may lead for a time to very close co-operation in pursuit of that object, does not necessarily imply any similarity or coincidence of motive, and still less any real sense of community among those who unite to pursue it. In the absence of profound dissimilarity of motive, it may easily engender a sense of community, and in doing so, may perhaps convert a several into an associative want. Thus, a group of farmers may associate purely because each sees in association a prospect of strengthening his economic position ; but, having acted together, the group may realise the benefits of associative action, and become inspired with the co-operative principle. Irish agriculture, under the guidance of A. E. and the *Irish Homestead*, has shown a marked tendency to pass from severalty of wants to associative wants.

Wants which are in their nature associative commonly imply a close, constant and continuing co-operation among the persons concerned, both until the object of the association has been secured, and thereafter for its exercise and maintenance. Those who pursue them therefore become far more easily imbued with the spirit of community, and the associations which are created for their fulfilment form a far more vital part of the structure of Society. Almost all the great and important associations which exercise a vital influence on affairs at the present time do so for one of two reasons. Either they exist, or are coming to exist, primarily for the fulfilment of associative wants, or they exercise influence, despite the severalty of the wants with which they are concerned, by reason of some extraneous pull, such as the possession by their members of vast wealth. In so far as associations are democratic, they can hardly exercise abiding influence unless their purposes are to a considerable extent associative.

It is perhaps necessary to illustrate the somewhat bare description given above by a few actual examples. A good instance of pure severalty of aim is to be found in any association which exists simply and solely to represent consumers. A Railway Season-Ticket Holders' Association, for instance, represents persons of the most diverse types, each of whom, broadly speaking, is solely concerned to get railway facilities for himself as cheaply as possible. A commercial or industrial company is another example. In a meeting of shareholders, broadly speaking, each individual is only concerned with the amount of dividend he will secure, and with the expectation of future dividends presented to him by the general position of the company. I do not mean, of course, that any individual acts in such an association purely as season-ticket holder or shareholder, or that his communal instincts and ideas find absolutely no play. That is not the case. But I do mean that the bond of the association itself is purely several, and that the fact of association carries with it no implication that the individuals associated have a common view as to the social position of season tickets or dividends in the community, or a common care for the satisfaction of each other's needs. Only if there is in the association some other bond besides that of pure severalty will the spirit of community be evoked, and the association take on a communal aspect.

This is not to say that associations based on pure severalty may not be useful parts of Society. But, as long as their basis remains purely several, they lack the necessary elements of community which will enable them to link up easily and enter into complementary relationship with the rest of Society. They have their part to play ; but it is an isolated and secondary part in the social fabric. How they act to-day we shall see more clearly when we come to consider social theory in its economic aspects. It is indeed in the economic sphere that such associations mainly, though not exclusively, appear on a large scale. In almost all other spheres, although associations based on severalty exist, they attain to importance only when their character of severalty is crossed by an associative want.

This very rough and preliminary analysis is sufficient to enable us to proceed to the task of definition. By an ' association ' I mean any group of persons pursuing a common purpose or system or aggregation of purposes by a course of co-operative action extending beyond a single act, and, for this purpose, agreeing together upon certain methods of procedure, and laying down, in however rudimentary a form, rules for common action. At least two things are fundamentally necessary to any association—a common purpose or purposes and, to a certain extent, rules of common action.

The primary condition of all association is a

common purpose ; for the object of all associations being the attainment of some end, there can be no association unless the attainment of that end is the purpose of the members. The ' end,' ' object,' or ' interest,' or as I prefer to call it, the ' purpose,' is the *raison d'être* of every association. But, while this is a fundamental point, it is important that it should not be pushed too far. The presence of a common purpose does not imply that it must be fully and consciously apprehended by all or, even in the case of already established associations, a majority of the members. Thus, an association may be constituted by its original founders with a definite purpose ; but, in course of time, the consciousness of this purpose may become blurred, and the association may survive almost purposelessly, men joining it rather because membership has become customary than for the attainment of any end. Some Churches are instances of such atrophied forms of association.

Secondly, it must be borne in mind that very many associations have, not a single, clearly definable purpose, but a number of purposes more or less intimately related one to another. In these cases, while, except in the circumstances contemplated above, each member is as a rule conscious of at least one of the purposes of the association, it does not follow that each member is conscious of, or shares in the desire to forward, each of the purposes in view. This may occur, either because a member does not fully appreciate the interrelation of the various purposes, and therefore fails to appreciate the significance of some of them, or because he does really differ from his fellows as to some of the purposes contemplated by the association, while agreeing with him about the rest, and feeling the association to be worth while for their sake alone. For example, when a Trade Union or an employers' association combines political and industrial activities, there will be some who, agreeing with the principal objects of the association and therefore desiring to remain members, will dissent from some of its purposes and methods. The Osborne Judgment controversy some years ago, and the recent controversy about the use of ' direct action ' for political purposes, alike served to force this issue to the front in the case of Trade Unions. It is perhaps unfortunate that it has not been similarly forced to the front in the case of employers' associations.

Thirdly, we must remember that associations are sustained by human beings, and are therefore capable of constant development. Changing circumstances, or a changing appreciation of the same circumstances, may impel the members of an association to widen or to narrow its objects, or to vary them from time to time. All associations possess a considerable elasticity in this respect, the degree of their elasticity varying largely with the amount of coherence they possess—which in turn depends mainly upon the intensity of the communal feeling which inspires them. But there is for every association a limit of elasticity, and, strained beyond this point by the inclusion of new purposes, the association will break, and a new one have to be created to fulfil the new purposes. The atrophy of the original purposes causes associations to decay. They may renew themselves by assuming new purposes ; but, if the change is too big or too violent, they break. Decay or breakage is the fate of every association in the end ; and as, from one cause or the other, associations disappear, men create new ones to take their place.

So much for the common purposes which are the moving and sustaining principle of all associations. But, as we saw, there is a secondary characteristic which is essential. Every association must, in some degree, prescribe common rules of action for its members. These rules may be very few and very rudimentary, and they commonly deal with the conduct of the members only in relation to the purposes of the association, though they often include written or unwritten moral rules of conduct designed to preserve the reputation of the association, and to act as a sort of elementary guarantee of personal honour. These rules generally include both general rules designed to cover particular cases as they arise, and particular directions issued by the governing body of the association for guidance in particular cases directly. With this aspect of the question we shall have to deal more fully when we consider, in a later chapter, the problems of democracy and representative government.

Our definition of the word ' association ' is clearly very wide indeed. It excludes momentary groups formed, without definite organisation, to carry out some single immediate object ; but it includes all organised groups possessed of a purpose entailing a course of action. It draws no distinction between groups whose purpose is in some sense political or social or communal, and groups whose purpose is purely sociable or recreational. It covers a football club or a dining club fully as much as a Church, a Trade Union or a political party.

Of course, it makes a great difference to the importance of an association, not only how far it is representative of those concerned in its purpose, but also how important its purpose is. But it is impossible to draw a theoretical line of distinction between associations which are 'social' and associations which are only sociable. For some practical purposes, as for representation upon public bodies, it is no doubt essential to draw such a distinction ; but it is necessary to recognise that, however drawn, it cannot be more than empirical. *All* associations are, in their various manners and degrees, parts of Society.

We can now turn to the word which, in the early part of this chapter, was so often used in close conjunction with the word 'association.' What is an *institution*, and in what sense is the word used in this book ? I find the thing for which the word stands difficult to define at all, and impossible to define in any but a largely negative manner. It is not, though it may manifest itself in or through, a group or association, nor has it, strictly speaking, any members. It does, of course, being a social thing, appear in, and operate through, human beings and associations ; but it depends for its institutional status, not upon a particular group of persons who are its members, frame its rules, and seek to effect through it a common purpose, but upon a general acceptance and recognition by the members of the community, backed by a sustaining force of custom or tradition, with or without the sanction of law. It is easily recognisable in some of its principal instances—marriage, monogamy, monarchy, peerage, caste, capitalism and many others belonging to different ages and civilisations.

But, side by side with this use of the word, there is another use of the word 'institution' which, while it suits well enough our everyday convenience, may easily be a source of confusion in a theoretical treatment of the question. The word 'institution' is often used to denote not only such ideas or relations as those instanced above, but also certain actual human groups which are, in the sense in which we have used the word, 'associations.' Thus Army, Navy, Church and State, to say nothing of less important bodies, are often directly referred to as 'institutions.'

It is important to notice that, in the sense in which we are using the word, Army, Navy, Church and State are not 'institutions,' but associations in which institutions may be held to be embodied or expressed. Thus the Church is an association in which the institution of religion is more or less perfectly embodied, the State an association more or less perfectly embodying the institution of political government, Army and Navy associations expressive of the institution of natural force, and so on.

Now, an idea is not an 'institution' merely because it is widely or generally held or accepted. It is an 'institution' only if, in addition to being so accepted, it is embodied in some external form of social structure or communal custom, either in

42

an association or in some actual form of social behaviour.

We may, then, provisionally define an 'institution' as a recognised custom or form of social tradition or idea, manifested in and through human beings either in their personal conduct and relationships or through organised groups or associations. Thus, the institution of monarchy is manifested in a king, and the social recognition accorded to him, the institution of peerage in the various peers and their status, the institution of marriage in the various married persons and their social recognition. In the second group of cases, the position appears to be rather different ; for there we first encounter a form of association and then recognise that its social status is due largely to the fact that it embodies an institution. In these cases, we have to study the association directly as an association, and then to study it further in its character as the embodiment of an institution.

An institution is, in fact, an idea which is manifested concretely in some aspect of social conduct, and which forms a part of the underlying assumptions of communal life. This does not make it permanent, or immune from decay or dissolution, though, as we shall see in a later chapter,[1] it does give to it an additional strength and power of survival. It can, however, change or decay. A monarchical Society may become a Republic, if it finds that the monarchical institution has outlived its use. The Guild System was in the Middle Ages the embodiment of an institution ; but the modern

[1] For a fuller treatment of the whole question, see Chapter XIII.

Companies which have descended from the Guilds have sunk down to the level of unimportant associations and have lost all claim to institutional status.

But, although institutions and their embodiments change, decay and die, it is characteristic of them to possess a greater degree of permanence than belongs to most associations. This relative permanence has both its good and its bad side. It helps to assure to an association or custom, which successfully embodies an idea found to be vital to the community, a greater stability than its members or its familiarity alone could assure to it, by giving it a communal sanction and status ; but it also tends to cause the survival of associations and customs which have acquired an institutional character long after they have ceased to be useful. Our estimate of the advantages and disadvantages of institutions will depend mainly upon our temperament. The temperamental Conservative (in no party sense) sees in institutions the bulwark of Society : the temperamental innovator sees in them the greatest barrier to progress.

We shall use the word ' institution ' in this book mainly in a rather narrower sense than has been here assigned to it. It will generally be used in conjunction with the word ' association ' to denote those institutions which are not, or are only in a secondary sense, embodied as associations. When I use it in the wider sense, to include institutions which are also embodied in associations, the context will make clear the sense, and I think no confusion will be created.

There is one further word which we must briefly

define before proceeding further. I have spoken repeatedly of *custom*. Perhaps this word hardly requires definition in the ordinary sense; for its meaning is sufficiently clear. It means no more and no less than a social habit or way of acting, common to the members of a community or social group, or at least widely enough diffused among them over a long enough period of time to have become in some degree taken for granted and acted upon in normal circumstances without any conscious exercise of deliberation. A custom is that which most men do naturally when placed in the appropriate circumstances. It is as vital to a community to have customs as it is vital to an individual to have instincts; for customs are to the community, as instincts are to the individual mind—labour-saving devices born of long use by successive generations.[1]

Customs, then, are a vital part of the being of community; but they do not, as customs, enter into the structure of Society—the organised part of the community. They enter into Society only when they become institutions, like marriage, or when their maintenance becomes a purpose to an association or institution. We shall therefore have little to say of them in this book, not because they are not important, but because, where they appear, they will appear largely under other forms.

Before I close this chapter, I must endeavour to clear away a difficulty which may easily have arisen in the reader's mind. I have spoken of the community as sustaining and of Society as being made

---

[1] Compare Samuel Butler's *Life and Habit* and Prof. James Ward's *Heredity and Memory*.

up of, associations and institutions, and of the latter as being, in different senses, within Society and within the community. Yet it is manifest that very many associations and institutions are international, and extend far beyond the boundaries of social area clearly recognisable as communities and social complexes which are clearly Societies. Does not this present a difficulty?

It will be seen that no difficulty is involved if our original discussion of community is borne in mind. We saw that two or more communities constantly claim the allegiance of a single imdividual. The family, the city, the nation, the group of closely related nations, the world—all these are communities. Every association or institution, however widespread, therefore exists within the area of some community. International association for specific purposes is the forerunner of a closer-knit international community, and can only exist because, in a rudimentary form, international community is already a fact.

Similarly, even international associations are within a Society, however rudimentary. They are the forerunners of a real Society of Nations which will be as necessary an expression of international community as Society within a nation is of national community. Internationally above all, free association helps to develop the sense of community on which it is based, and to forward the creation of an international social complex for the expression of that community.

CHAPTER III

THE PRINCIPLE OF FUNCTION

ALTHOUGH our last chapter was concerned primarily with definitions, a number of important conclusions have emerged from it. We have learnt to regard community as a complex of individuals, associations, institutions and customs in varied and multiform relationships : we have learnt to regard Society as a complex of associations and institutions expressing, not the whole of the communal life, but that part of it which is organised ; and we have learnt to see in associations bodies created by the wills of individuals for the expression and fulfilment of purposes which they have in common. We have, in fact, already penetrated the essential and underlying structure of social life.

There is, however, at least one point of ultimate principle in relation to which our vision is still fundamentally incomplete. Our method has forced us so far to look at each form of social structure in something like isolation from the others. We have analysed and defined ; but we have not, except in relation to community, as yet made clear the structural principle which makes the complexities of social life into something at least approaching a

47

coherent whole. The underlying principle of community, indeed, is neither more nor less than community itself—the sense of unity and social brotherhood which permeates a mass of men and women and makes them, in a real sense, one. But we have not seen what is the underlying principle of *social organisation*, a principle which must be distinct from the principle of community, however dependent upon it. This principle is the principle of *Function*.

Most people know something of those ethical theories which, from the time of Plato onwards, have made 'function' their governing principle. In ethics the principle is that each individual should seek not his own self-interest as such, nor his own self-development or self-expression as such, but the fulfilment of his function in the social whole of which he forms a part. His 'end' is not to be an isolated or purely personal end, but an end which at once places him in relation to something beyond himself. Pushed to an extreme, this theory may easily result not merely in a denial of all democracy, but in a denial of personality itself as an ultimate or 'end,' in a glorification and personification of Society in which human values are largely lost, and the personal aspects of life rigidly subordinated to the collective elements. 'Function' is eminently unsatisfactory as an ethical principle, that is, as *the* principle which should determine individual conduct, not because each individual has not, in a very real sense, his function to fulfil, but because he has so many various functions, and because it is just in the choice of and between functions and in assigning their relative places to the many functions, social and personal, of which we are conscious, that our selfhood appears as a co-ordinating principle beyond any of them.

But the fact that function is not *the* paramount ethical principle does not mean that it is not the paramount principle of social organisation. We have seen that men make, and enter into, associations for the purpose of satisfying common wants, that is, in terms of action, for the execution of common purposes. Every such purpose or group of purposes is the basis of the *function* of the association which has been called into being for its fulfilment. Again, every institution in Society has an object which has determined the main lines of its growth. The fulfilment of this object is, then, the necessary basis of the function of the institution. Of course, either an association or an institution may be itself complex and have a variety of related purposes or objects, and therefore perhaps a variety of related functions. But as the purpose or object behind an association or institution must be specific and in some degree intelligible in order to have the power to call the association or institution into being, so the functions of all associations and institutions, however they may change and develop, are, in the last resort, also specific.

This is the reason why the functional principle is finally applicable to associations and institutions, but not to individuals. Every individual is in his nature universal : his actions and courses of action, his purposes and desires, are specific because he makes them so ; but he himself is not, and cannot be, made specific, and therefore cannot be expressed in terms of function. This essential difference makes once more manifest the falsity of the parallel that is often drawn between individuals and associations. An association is not, and cannot be, in any real sense, a ' person,' because it is specific and functional, and not universal. The individual becomes ' functional,' or rather ' multi-functional,' only by limiting himself ; the association is functional and limited by its very nature.

But function is not so much the final cause of each separate association, as the principle underlying the unity and coherence of associations. We have seen that the value and full development of Society depends not only on the wide prevalence and diffusion of association in the Commonwealth, but also on the successful co-operation and coherence of the various associations. The possibility of this coherence depends upon the fulfilment by each association of its social function. In so far as the various associations fulfil their respective social purposes, and in so far as these purposes are themselves complementary and necessary for social well-being, the welter of associations in the community is converted into a coherent Society. In so far as the associations work irrespective of their function in a social whole, or set before themselves purposes which are mutually contradictory and irreconcilable with the good of the whole, the development out of the welter of associations of a coherent Society is thwarted and retarded.

It will be observed that a new consideration has been introduced into the argument in the course of the preceding paragraph. In treating function as

THE PRINCIPLE OF FUNCTION

the characteristic, not of an isolated association, but of an association as a factor in a coherent social whole, or at least a social whole capable of coherence, we have introduced a consideration of value which compels us to scrutinise the purpose of each particular association in the light of its communal value in and for the whole.

This consideration is, of course, in no sense novel. The point is clearly stated, although the implications of it are not clearly realised, in Rousseau's *Discourse on Political Economy* in the following words : [1]—

"Every political Society is composed of other smaller societies of different kinds, each of which has its interests and rules of conduct ; but those societies which everybody perceives, because they have an external and authorised form, are not the only ones which actually exist in the community: all individuals who are united by a common interest compose as many others, temporary or permanent, whose influence is none the less real because it is less apparent, and the proper observation of whose relations is the true knowledge of public morals and manners."

Thus, if we view an association as an isolated unit, its object can be only the fulfilment of whatever purpose or purposes its members have created and maintain it to fulfil. Its will is, in Rousseau's sense, 'general' [2] in relation to the members of

[1] Rousseau, *Political Economy*, my (*Everyman*) edition, p. 253.

[2] The use of the word 'general' in this connexion must not be understood as contradicting, what was said earlier, that the function of every association is 'specific' and not 'general.' Its purpose and function remain 'specific,' whether the will behind it be 'general' or 'particular.'

51

the association, but ' particular ' in relation to the community as a whole.

The members of an association, as we have seen, can only come together and work together in the association if they have, to a certain extent, a common object or purpose. Clearly, such a purpose may be one that is socially desirable, or it may be one that hardly affects any person outside the association for either good or ill, or it may be definitely anti-social. The mere fact that the association seeks only the ' interest ' of its own members (as, if the word ' interest ' is understood in a wide enough sense, every association, like every individual, must do), is not enough to make it anti-social, or to prevent it from being socially desirable. It is for the good of the community that each group within it should keep itself amused, instructed, developed ; for these goods of individuals are, so far, clear additions to the common stock of happiness, which can only be the happiness of individuals. An association becomes anti-social not in seeking the good of its own members, but in seeking their good in ways which detract from the good of others. Such detraction only occurs either when one association's objects come into conflict with those of another, so that both cannot be fully satisfied, or when an association aims at an object which conflicts with the personal objects of some individual, whether a member of the association or not. Wherever such a conflict occurs, coherence is impaired, and the complementary working of associations and individuals is made less perfect. The existence of conflict shows that something is wrong ; but it does not, of course, show on which side the wrong lies, or how it is distributed between the two.

We seem here to be confronted with a difficulty. We cannot accept the objects of each association, just as its members have made them, as making for a coherent Society and a development of the sense of community. It is, indeed, manifest that very many associations, in seeking a partial good for their own members, are acting anti-socially and impairing the coherence of Society as a whole. We must, therefore, criticise and value associations in accordance with some definite standard.

The term 'function' is in itself, as applied to associations, a reference to such a standard of value; for it places each association in relation, not only to its own members, but to other associations and institutions, that is, to Society, and also to individuals—to both the organised and the un-organised parts of social life, that is, to Community. If our first question in relation to any association must be, 'What are the purposes which this association was created and is maintained by its members to subserve?' we ask that question only in order to be able the better to proceed at once to a second question, 'What is the function which this association can serve in Society and in community?'

This does not mean, of course, that it is possible arbitrarily to determine from outside what the function of an association is. The first question is no less essential than, and is essential to, the second. A 'function' can only be based upon a purpose. If men have formed an association for one purpose, we cannot properly tell them that its function is to

53

do something quite different which has never entered into their heads. The fact that the purposes of men in associations change and develop does indeed enable us to some extent to anticipate changes and developments, and to say that an association will find its true function by proceeding along a line of development along which it has already begun to move. But, apart from such intelligent anticipations, we are limited in assigning to any association its function to the purposes which its members have set before themselves in creating and maintaining it.

Social purposes are, thus, the raw material of social functions, and social functions are social purposes selected and placed in coherent relationship. This selection cannot have a purely scientific basis ; for it is a matter of ends as well as means, and depends upon individual standards of value and the kind of social life which the individual desires. Thus at this, as at every other fundamental point of social theory, we are driven back upon the individual consciousness and judgment as the basis of all social values. Mr. Colvin of the *Morning Post* regards one kind of social life as finally desirable, and I another. There is a sense in which I believe most firmly that I am right and he is wrong ; but social theory cannot reconcile that fundamental difference between us which is a difference of ends, though it may clear away misunderstandings and prevent loose thinking on both sides.

Each of us has in his mind, whether we rationalise and systematise it or not, some conception of the sort of social life which is ultimately desirable. Our conceptions of the functions of particular

THE PRINCIPLE OF FUNCTION

associations are inevitably formed in the light of our ultimate conception of social value. In laying bare the basis of community it should be possible for men of varying standards and temperaments to agree ; but I am fully conscious that in the later chapters of this book I shall inevitably, as I come to deal with more concrete subjects, more and more obtrude my own standards of valuation. I can lay bare the functional basis of association without bringing my temperament into the argument ; but as soon as I begin to deal with the actual function of any particular association there will certainly be wigs on the green.

That point in the argument, however, we have not yet reached. We must first carry a good deal further our examination of the principle of function in its general application. Function, we have seen, emerges clearly when, and only when, an association is regarded, not in isolation, but in relation to other associations and to individuals, that is, to some extent in relation to a system of associations, a Society, and a system of associations and individuals, a community. Such a system evidently implies a more or less clear demarcation of spheres as between the various functional associations, in order that each may make its proper contribution to the whole without interfering with the others. It is, however, easy, in search of symmetry, to push this point too far. It is essential that the main lines of demarcation should be laid down, and, in the case of the more vital forms of association, that they should be most carefully and exactly drawn, wherever possible by experience rather than by arbitrary constitution-making '; but in the case of the less vital forms of association, which affect the general structure of Society only in a small degree either for good or for ill, the same exact delimitation of spheres is unnecessary, and even undesirable as detracting from the freedom and spontaneity of association.

We must indeed bear in mind always that associations are not mere machines, but are capable of growth and development. We must not, therefore, even in the case of the most vital associations, so exactly define their function and sphere of operation for to-day as to prevent them from developing the power to exercise their function of to-morrow. If we do, the result will not be in most cases what we expect. The association will develop in spite of prohibition ; but in developing it may well break the Society which encloses it, or at the least cause vast waste of energy and unnecessary friction. We must remember always that it is of vital importance for a community not to be compelled constantly to make for itself new sets of associations, but rather to develop out of old ones the changed forms which are required for the fulfilment of new functions. It is this vital need of community that makes it so important to preserve as far as possible the freedom of association and the greatest spontaneity of associative action that is consistent with social coherence.

There are, of course, risks attaching to this course. If association is left largely free and untrammelled, many associations, instead of fulfilling their function in the social whole, will concern themselves to a considerable extent in fulfilling even the anti-social

THE PRINCIPLE OF FUNCTION

purposes of their members, or in doing something which, while it is in itself not anti-social but even socially valuable, falls within the function of some other form of association. There arise in this way two main forms of *perversion* of function, leading respectively to *opposition* and to *confusion* in Society. These two forms of perversion cannot, of course, be kept clearly distinct ; for they often appear together in the same association and in the same act. They are, however, theoretically distinct, and we can, at the outset, examine them separately.

Opposition arises, as we have seen, when an association pursues a purpose which, being a purpose of its own members,[1] is anti-social in that it not only conflicts with the purposes of other associations or individuals, but with the good of the community. Opposition, then, arises from the pursuit of anti-social purposes. Strictly speaking, no anti-social purpose can be a part of the function of an association, in the sense in which we are using the term ' function.' But, as a function is always a complex thing, the element of ' opposition ' may arise in the course of the pursuit of a socially desirable function. Thus, the production of commodities for use and the preservation of order are both socially desirable functions ; but either of them may be pursued in anti-social ways which give rise to ' opposition ' and perversion of function. If an association producing commodities for use makes its main object not the production

[1] Or, of course, of an effective majority or effective ' conscious minority ' of them.

57

for use, but the realisation of a profit for its members, perversion of function arises. Commodities are still produced ' for use ' in a sense ; but the function of the association is perverted by the introduction of the profit-making purpose. Similarly, if an association whose function is the preservation of order preserves order in the interest of a single class and deals unequal justice to rich and poor, law and order are still partially preserved ; but the function of the association is perverted by its partiality and the foundations of justice are to some extent undermined. We shall have much more to say of this subject when we come to consider the economic structure of Society and the problem of class-divisions within the community.

Confusion arises when two associations attempt to fulfil the same purpose, and when the purpose is such as requires not a multiplicity of doers, but doing on a co-ordinated plan. Such confusion may be perfectly *bona fide* and even fortuitous. There are functions which lie on the border-line of two or more associations, but which must be· fulfilled by only one if confusion is to be avoided. Again, there are many cases in which two or more associations, whose purposes were originally distinct, develop towards the same object, and become wholly or partly identical in function. Such cases are often dealt with by amalgamation ; but failing this or an agreed re-allocation of functions, confusion arises. Again, in many cases there is some job which badly needs doing, and two or more groups of men simultaneously conceive the idea of forming an association for the doing of it. Here again amalgamation is often the obvious remedy. Many other cases can easily be brought to mind in which confusion of functions arises even where the purposes of the associations concerned are admitted to be socially desirable or not harmful.

Mingled *confusion* and *opposition*, involving a double perversion of function, is very frequent. Let us return to our case of the production of commodities. Under the existing economic order of Society, there is more than one party to such production. Employers and workers are alike strongly, and separately, organised in economic associations. Very often the employers in a given industry and the workers in that industry are endeavouring to secure the adoption of diametrically opposite policies in relation to the same thing. Their purposes are opposed, and, without entering into the moral factors in the situation, we can see that this often leads to perversion of the function of the association by way both of opposition and of confusion. That is to say, both associations seek to cover to some extent the same field of activity and this leads to confusion, even if their points of view are not fundamentally opposed ; but often in addition each advocates a different policy, so that not only confusion, but also actual conflict, results.

It is important to notice that perversion of function in one case, especially where the perversion gives rise to actual opposition, frequently leads to, and even necessitates, perversion of function in other cases. If the appropriate organisation is not fulfilling a particular function, it may become necessary or desirable for some other organisation, less fitted by its nature for the task, to undertake to fulfil it as best it can. Again, if one association is fulfilling its function in a perverted manner, so as to serve a sectional instead of a general interest, it may be necessary or desirable for some other organisation to intervene in order to redress the balance. Current controversies about the use of direct action (*i.e.* the strike) for political purposes serve to illustrate this point. It is contended by many of the advocates of direct action that the perversion of function on the part of the State makes it necessary for the Trade Unions to act in the industrial field in order to counteract the effects of this political perversion. It falls outside the scope of our present inquiry to determine whether this argument is sound or not in any particular case; but it is clear that such cases can and do arise.

At the same time, it must always be remembered that perversion of functions is always, in itself, a bad thing, whether it is spontaneous perversion or consequential perversion designed to counteract a perversion which has already taken place. It may be necessary in certain cases; but the mere fact of its necessity is a clear indication that all is not well with Society. When Society is in health, each association fulfils its social function with the minimum of perversion.

Indeed, when counteracting forms of perversion become necessary on any large scale, they serve as a clear indication that the structure of Society requires to be overhauled. Perversion, carried to an extreme, and accompanied by its counteracting forms leads to revolution, followed by a reconstruction of the body social. Such revolution can, of course, be more or less complete ; and involve a more or less complete reconstructing and a more or less complete 'sweep' of the old social régime. Often, less degrees of perversion and counter-perversion compel a readjustment of social organisation without the need for a general evolution in the body social. The first so - called 'revolution' in Russia was rather such a readjustment than a real revolution ; but, this proving inadequate, it was followed by the 'November Revolution,' which was a real revolution involving a fundamental reconstruction of Society.

It is impossible to study the forms of functional perversion with any completeness without a fairly thorough examination of the problem of social classes, which has been responsible, at least in recent times, for by far the greatest amount of perversion. It is also impossible to make the study complete without dealing with the position of organised religion, *i.e.* Churches, in Society ; for religious differences have been, at least in former times, almost equally potent causes of perversion. Both these points, however, must be reserved for later consideration. In this chapter, our object has been merely that of laying bare the functional principle itself, on the basis on which Society, as a complex of associations and institutions, must rest if it is to achieve any degree of coherence or to make possible a real and abiding spirit of community. Perversion of function, by destroying the coherence of social organisation, not only upsets the balance of Society, but stirs up bad blood between the members of the community, and thereby impairs that part of the life of the individual which falls outside the sphere of social organisation, almost equally with that part which falls within it. Due performance by each association of its social function, on the other hand, not only leads to smooth working and coherence in social organisation, but also removes the removable social hindrances to the ' good life ' of the individual. In short, function is the key not only to ' social,' but also to communal and personal well-being.

CHAPTER IV

THE FORMS AND MOTIVES OF ASSOCIATION

THE time has now come for a more thorough examination of the forms of association which exist in Society, and for some further discussion of the social character of the motives underlying association. I do not mean that an exhaustive enumeration of the forms of association, or even an exhaustive classification of them, is either possible or desirable—still less that the motives behind association can be satisfactorily reduced to a few broad and simple categories. The object of this chapter is essentially tentative. I shall only try to enumerate and classify the main forms of association—those which possess the greatest degree of social content, and to discuss briefly those dominant social motives which are constantly appearing in many diverse forms of association.

Even apart from the limitations of our space and time, there is one fact which would by itself forbid any exhaustive catalogue. Social association is forever assuming new forms and discarding old ones, as new problems emerge for men to deal with, and as men change their attitude towards the problems which confront them. The fountain of association does not run dry, and it is impossible to enumerate all those who come to drink of its waters. Moreover, if we could enumerate to-day, our list would be out of date to-morrow; for new forms of association would have arisen which very possibly would not fit into any classification which we might have devised on the basis of our present knowledge.

Nevertheless, we can usefully proceed to a classification of a sort. While new forms of association are constantly arising, the essential forms of association only vary over considerable periods. That even the most essential forms do vary, appear and disappear, cannot be denied. There have been many independent communities without a State; yet to most people to-day the State appears to be an essential form of association. The Guilds were an essential form in the Middle Ages; but where are the Guilds to-day? It is true that we have to-day instead of craft Guilds many other forms of economic association; but is even economic association an essential form for all communities? Have there not been communities devoid of *distinct* economic organisation? This can only be denied by those who persist, in face of all vital considerations, in regarding the family in certain primitive Societies as *primarily* and distinctly an economic association. The family in these Societies certainly had economic, among other, functions; but this is not enough to constitute it as, in its fundamental character, an economic association.

We must recognise, then, not only that the forms of association vary constantly from day to day, but also that even the essential forms vary over longer periods. Our classification therefore has reference, not to all social situations, but to the social situation of the civilised communities of our own day. Even so it is necessarily imperfect ; for the institutions of revolutionised Russia and Hungary require, in some respects, a new classification, and a revolution elsewhere in civilised countries may compel a general amendment of the classification which is adopted here. The nearer we approach in this book to the study of actual social organisations, the more limited and inadequate we shall necessarily find our generalisations to become.

It will be a part of our object in this chapter, not merely to describe the outstanding forms of association in our own day and generation, but to attempt, to some extent, to discriminate between essential and non-essential forms. This is, of course, a matter of degree, and no definite line can be drawn. There are, however, apart from doubtful cases, certain forms of association which can fitly be described as essential to Society, and certain others which are not essential to Society. It must be made clear at the outset that this discrimination does not imply any moral valuation. All associations must finally be judged and valued by their service to the individuals who are members of the community, and it may well be found that some of the associations which are here classified as non-essential are of transcendent value to the individual. This, however, is not the question with which I am here concerned. It is purely with *social* essentiality that our classification deals. That is to say,

AN INTRODUCTION TO SOCIAL THEORY

a part of my present purpose is to discriminate between those associations which form an integral part of the organised coherence of Society, from those which, however great their value, are not in this sense integral and essential to organised Society. The meaning and purpose of this discrimination will emerge more clearly at a later stage.

We may reasonably expect to find the essential forms of association among those forms which are outstanding, and occur to the mind naturally as typical forms. It does not follow by any means that all outstanding forms are essential: I have only said that essential forms are likely to be outstanding. We must begin, then, with at least a partial classification of outstanding forms.

This classification cannot be entirely simple in character; for there are two different principles on which it must be based. We have to consider both (a) the *content* of the interest which the association sets before itself; and (b) its method of operation in relation to that interest. The first of these principles is of supreme importance in revealing the interrelation in Society of the various forms of association, that is, their specific functions; the second is of primary importance in discriminating between essential and non-essential forms.

According to the first of these two ways of classification, we have to distinguish between associations according to the content of their various interests. Here the chief forms which emerge at once into view are the *political*, the *vocational* and *appetitive*, the *religious*, the *provident*, the *philanthropic*, the *sociable*, and the *theoretic*. There are others; but

THE FORMS OF ASSOCIATION

most of the prevalent forms of association fall under one or another of these heads.

Of some of the more important forms of *political* association we shall have much more to say in the next chapter, when we deal with the State and kindred forms of association and institution. We must, however, say something of them here. By a *political* association I mean an association of which the main purpose is to deal with those personal relationships which arise directly out of the fact that men live together in communities, and which require, and are susceptible to, social organisation. I freely admit that it is almost impossible to define accurately or clearly the nature and functions of political association, and I must make it plain that nothing that is said in this chapter is intended to prejudge the question, discussed in the next chapter, whether the State, for instance, can be regarded as a purely *political* association in the sense here given to the word. That is a very big question indeed ; but it does not affect the present issue. I am here, and throughout this book, using the term 'political' in a definite and limited sense, in which it is contrasted with vocational, religious and other functional terms.

A *political* association, then, is an association of which the purposes and interests are primarily 'political' in the sense defined above. This definition includes not only the State *qua* association, and the various less extensive regional and local authorities operating as political bodies within the geographical area included in a State, but also, as we shall see, in a secondary sense, many other forms of association which are also 'political' in their interest—a political party or society or any bodies concerned with the advocacy of any form of political doctrine or policy. Parliament, and the County Borough of Smethwick, in so far as they are associations, fall, in this classification, under the same heading as the Liberal Party or the Anti-Vaccination League.

A *vocational* association may be defined as an association consisting of persons who are and whose purpose or interest in the association is directly and primarily concerned with the production, distribution or exchange of some commodity, or the rendering of some service, or with some question or course of action directly subordinate to one or more of these interests. It thus includes the whole range of professional and occupational association, from that of manual workers to that of technicians and experts, and to that of employers and traders and capitalists. A Trade Union, a professional institute or society, an Employers' Association, a Limited Company, the British Empire Producers' Organisation, the British Medical Association, and the National Union of Teachers are all instances of vocational association.

It will have been noticed that, in the preliminary list of the main forms of association under this classification, vocational association was specially linked with another form, which, for want of a better word, I am forced to call *appetitive*. It must be made clear at once that the word is not used in any bad or derogatory sense. By appetitive associations I mean those bodies whose members' primary concern in the association is not, as in the case of

THE FORMS OF ASSOCIATION

vocational associations, with production or the rendering of service, but with *consumption and use,* that is, with the securing of a supply on fair terms of the commodities produced and the services rendered by, or under the auspices of, vocational associations. The consumers' Co-operative Movement, the Railway Season-Ticket Holders' Association, the Commercial Gas Users' Association, and the Parents' National Educational Union are all examples of *appetitive* association. This form, it will readily be seen, is mainly complementary to *vocational* association, the two forms corresponding to the double relations of buying and selling, demand and supply, receiving and giving. Different schools of social propagandists lay very different stresses upon the relative importance of these two complementary forms of association.

It is perhaps necessary barely to notice here a point which will be more fully dealt with in later chapters. There are certain schools of thought which regard the State, and with it the local authorities, as primarily associations of consumers and users, that is to say as, in our sense, *appetitive* associations. Similarly, some schools of Communists regard the Commune as primarily an association of producers and service renderers, that is, in our sense, a vocational association. These theories lead directly to different views as to the proper constitution of State or Commune ; but, as they do not affect our present classification, consideration of them can be postponed till a later stage.

We come next to those forms of association which can be called *religious.* These include not only organised Churches and Connexions, but also propagandist movements which aim at securing a religious object, such as the 'Life and Liberty Movement' within the Church of England. As we shall have much more to say of them later, they need not detain us here.

The next important form of association is the *provident*, in which a number of persons join together for mutual assistance, whether under a definite scheme of contributions and benefits for certain purposes, or for a less rigid and definite form of mutual help or beneficence. A Friendly Society, or other *mutual* insurance associations, whether among workers or among capitalists in a particular trade (*e.g.* shipping), or among teachers or clergymen, or on a basis which takes no account of occupation, falls under this head. Many Insurance Companies are, of course, not provident and mutual, but profit-making concerns, which belong to the sphere of vocational organisation ; but the great Friendly Societies with their millions of members afford a large-scale example of real provident associations. Trade Unions also are, of course, in their aspect of benefit societies, assignable to this class of association.

Closely allied to provident associations in certain respects, though very different from them in others, are the many associations which exist not for the securing of benefits for their own members, but for the conferring of benefits on other people. Charitable Societies of whatever type, whether they actually confer benefits or merely meddle with other people's affairs, and associations which deal with moral

THE FORMS OF ASSOCIATION

rather than material benefits for others, can be grouped together under this head. *Philanthropic* will serve for a name for this very mixed class.

Next comes what is perhaps the largest of all groups of associations, those of a purely or mainly *sociable* character. These are found in their pure form in the vast number of football clubs, cricket clubs, athletic associations, whist clubs, dancing clubs, workmen's clubs, ' clubmen's ' clubs, night clubs, and all the other types of associations devoted purely to objects of sport, recreation and sociability. Mixed forms are also frequently found. Constitutional clubs, Liberal Clubs, Labour Clubs and many others are sociable in character, but are confined to persons holding similar opinions, and partake in some small degree of the nature of political associations. Purely sociable associations often federate with other associations of the same kind ; but generally speaking they are, if their federations and tournaments are included, sufficient unto themselves. Except when licensing or gaming laws are under consideration, or some particularly ardent campaign for public morality is in progress, they mix little, as a rule, in the affairs of Society.

All the forms of association mentioned above are in a definite sense practical and aim at the taking of certain overt forms of action, whether administrative propagandist, or purely recreative. This is not the case with the only remaining form of association with which we shall here concern ourselves, the *theoretical* form. This includes learned and scientific societies of every type, whatever their object of study and discussion. As learning and science have a definite bearing on many practical affairs, theoretic associations often tend to approximate to one or another of the practical types, or to possess a mixed character. Moreover, vocational associations, especially among technicians concerned with a common body of knowledge, often pursue theoretical as well as practical ends. Many discuss both the economic and other claims of their members and the status of their profession, and also the theoretic aspects of the science which they profess. Again, the close relation between industry and science gives rise to associations, half practical and half theoretical, concerned with the application of scientific results and methods to industrial problems. The numerous Industrial Research Associations which have sprung up in recent years are examples of this hybrid form.

So far we have been following entirely the first of the two principles of classification with which we set out—and distinguishing associations according to the *content* of their respective interests. We have now to take up our other principle, and to survey associations briefly according to their method of operation. We saw, in speaking of political, and again of religious, associations, that they included not only such bodies as States and Churches respectively, but also all manner of other societies, the content of whose purpose was political or religious. Our second principle will make plain the difference between, say, a State and a political party, or the Church of England and the ' Life and Liberty Movement ' which aims at its regeneration. The difference in both those cases is that

THE FORMS OF ASSOCIATION

States and Churches are alike mainly *administrative*, whereas political parties and movements among Churchmen are mainly *propagandist*.

By an *administrative* association I mean an association which is primarily concerned, not with the advocacy of any particular opinion, but with the doing of some particular job, the arranging and conducting of some particular part of the work which has to be done in Society. This work may be done in many different ways and with many varying degrees of success. Thus the State may be governed by the Unionist Party, the Liberal Party, or the Labour Party, or by a Coalition ; but the primary concern of the State is not with Toryism or Liberalism or Labour, but with the doing of certain definite jobs—with the work to be done, and not with the ways of doing it.

All the forms of association mentioned in our previous classification include *administrative* associations, which are indeed primary in every group. Not only States and Churches, but also Trade Unions, Limited Companies, cricket clubs, Friendly Societies, charitable associations, scientific societies, Co-operative Societies and the rest are principally *administrative* in function, that is to say, they exist not for the spreading of opinion, but for the doing of things. In a very real sense, administrative associations are primary, where propagandist associations are only secondary, and it is among the administrative associations that we shall find the *essential* social associations of which we are in search.

Propagandist associations have already been defined by inference. They are those associations which exist not so much for the doing of a particular job, as for advocating that the job should be done in a particular way, that a particular policy or constitution should be adopted by the primary association concerned with the doing of it. Propagandist associations are secondary, because they exist, not in order to do things themselves, but to persuade primary associations and individuals into a particular course of action. There is thus a sense in which they aim at their own extinction; for, when their policy is completely adopted, they cease to have a reason for existence, unless they find a new policy or remain in being in order to see that the results already achieved are maintained. They may, as a whole, be very necessary to Society; but no particular propagandist association is essential to the structure of Society.

Of course, I am not denying that all associations, however propagandist, possess, in a secondary sense, an administrative character, or that most administrative associations also partake, in a similar sense, of the propagandist character. But the distinction none the less holds; for the fact that no association at all can exist without being confronted by internal administrative problems does not make the main purpose of the association administrative. Similarly, the fact that an association engages in certain forms of propagandist activity does not give it a propagandist character. The projected establishment of a Propaganda Department of State would not make the State a mainly propagandist association.

We are now in a position to pursue rather further

THE FORMS OF ASSOCIATION

our quest of the essential forms of social association, not necessarily those essential for all time, but those essential in our own day and civilisation. It has already been made clear that the term ' essential ' is not meant simply to imply any moral valuation, and that it is purely *social* essentiality with which we are here concerned. The key to essentiality is thus the performance of some function which is vital to the coherent working of Society, and without which Society would be lop-sided or incomplete. We have seen that no particular propagandist association can be regarded as essential in this sense ; for, although propaganda performs a highly desirable function in keeping individuals and associations ' up to the scratch,' they are not themselves concerned with the direct execution of vital social functions. Propagandist association in general is, no doubt, essential ; but no particular propagandist association can claim essentiality except under one condition.

This condition is the atrophy or perversion of an essential administrative association or institution. Where this occurs, and the administrative body fails to perform its function, propagandist organisation may be, for the moment, the only way of recalling it to its function or, failing that, calling a new body into being in its place. The propagandist association is not, and can hardly become, this new body ; but it may be temporarily essential as a means.

This, however, is only a partial exception to a rule which holds good in general. It is among administrative associations that the essential forms must be sought. But not all such forms of association are essential. Society can do without any particular form of sociable association, as it can do without any propagandist association, and although it cannot do without sociable association as a whole. The same applies to provident and philanthropic and also to theoretic associations. Religious association, on the other hand, must probably be regarded as essential to almost every existing Society, because religion as a personal emotion and belief is widely diffused in almost every existing community. The position of religious associations in Society is, however, as we shall see later, peculiar because of their fundamentally and exclusively spiritual function.[1]

We are left with the three forms of political, vocational and appetitive association. Each of these must, I think, be regarded as essential. Each deals with a vital aspect of Social organisation, with an ' interest ' vital to the mass of the members of the community, and each is based upon a deep-rooted and vital instinct of association. It is mainly on the right relationship of these three forms of association that the coherent organisation of Society depends. I cannot hope to make this point absolutely clear at the present stage ; but I believe that it will emerge with increasing clearness in the course of subsequent chapters.

Even if we hold that a particular *form* of association is essential, this is not by itself enough to establish the essentiality of any single association belonging to that class. Within each of the essential forms we may expect to find, in any particular stage of social development, certain actual associations

[1] See Chapter XI.

which can be regarded as essential ; but, in order to establish this, it is necessary to consider not only the form of any association in question, but also its particular content and the motives which animate its members in their common action. Not every association which is administrative in character and political in content is sufficiently important to merit the character of essentiality. For this it must have a particular function which is vital enough to substantiate its claim. Thus, the State may be an essential association ; but, to take an extreme instance, it is by no means clear that the unnatural aggregation which we call a Rural District Council can claim the same privilege. Again, in the vocational sphere, it is essential that producers should be organised ; but it does not follow that each particular Trade Union or Employers' Association can claim essentiality. The final test of essentiality is practical, and cannot be made by any abstract or scientific procedure.

There is, however, one further important test to which associations for essentiality can be subjected. In our preliminary discussion of the nature of association,[1] we attempted a distinction between different types of motive which animate men in association. We drew a distinction between ' several ' and ' associative ' motives, and discussed in some detail the bearings of this distinction on the social import of associations. We saw that ' associative ' wants and motives far more easily engendered a sense of community than ' several ' wants, and therefore gave the association animated

[1] See ante, p. 34.

by them a higher status and made it, so far, a greater factor in the making of Society. Our subsequent examination of the main forms of association has placed us in a position to appreciate more fully the bearing of this distinction upon social theory, and also to develop it somewhat further.

The mere fact that an association is animated mainly by truly ' associative ' motives and interests is not enough to establish the fact that it is fulfilling a useful function in Society. For the ' associative ' want which it seeks to fulfil, however ' associative ' it may be, is so far only a want of the members of the association, and may still be contrary to the general interest of the community. An ' associatively ' motived association, therefore, is not necessarily a socially useful association. But as it is the case that there is such a thing as general social well-being, it is clear that the interests of the members of a community do run together more than they clash. The members of a community have, *ex hypothesi*, a sense of unity and social relationship, and, while they often organise in groups which are opposed on particular points, there is a *prima facie* reason for supposing that, in the majority of cases, where they co-operate on an associative basis for the fulfilling of a want which they can only enjoy in common, the fulfilment of that want is in the general interest. Moreover, as the community can only find an organised expression—even so always a partial expression—through social associations and institutions, it is clear that associations based on an associative want must be the main ingredients in the Society. In

THE FORMS OF ASSOCIATION

them, men learn to co-operate closely and constantly; and close and constant co-operation in the joint fulfilment of a common object, though it is not necessarily to be identified with the fulfilment of a socially useful function, is the chief means by which men can learn how to fulfil such functions.

It is not, however, generally possible to discriminate sharply between associations or forms of associations, and to say that in this association or form the basis is purely 'several,' and in the other, purely 'associative.' Almost every association is, as we have seen, a medley of different motives, and is partly 'several,' and only in part truly 'associative.' But, in proportion as an association finds and fulfils its function in Society, the 'associative' basis tends to become predominant, and the motive of 'severalty' sinks into the background. The best instance I can find of this may strike many readers as being highly controversial; but I cite as clearly illustrating my meaning and expressing my own profound belief. A Trade Union used to be defined as "a continuous association of wage-earners for the purpose of maintaining or improving their conditions of employment." Such a definition almost implies the complete dominance of 'severalty' in the motives animating the members of the association. But, in our own day, whatever its justification in the past, this definition has become clearly inadequate; for the increasing tendency of Trade Unionists to claim for their associations not merely better conditions, but a definite place in the control of industry, plainly implies an emergence of truly 'associative' motives, and, in my own opinion,

79

represents a substantial development of Trade Unionism towards the performance of its proper social function.

Be this as it may, it is clear that, as an association changes and develops, it may change its motives as well as its purposes, and may pass from a stage in which ' severalty ' is predominant to one in which it is mainly actuated by ' associative ' motives. This is an indication, though it is not a proof, that the association is moving towards the discovery of its true function in Society.

This chapter has dealt entirely with the forms and motives of association, and has only once or twice cursorily mentioned the working of institutions as distinct from associations. I have made this omission advisedly, not because institutions are not important, but because we have not yet reached the stage at which it is possible to deal adequately with them. This we shall be able to do only when we have examined successively the political, vocational and appetitive (especially the economic), and religious structure of Society, in which institutions mainly appear. Upon this part of our inquiry we can now embark without further delay.

CHAPTER V

THE STATE

W HAT is the State ?   And what is its function in Society and in the community ?   These questions appear to us already in a different light from that in which they appear in most books on Social Theory.   They are still vital problems ; but they are no longer the centre of the whole problem of community.   The State, however important, is and can be for us no more than the greatest and most permanent association or institution in Society, and its claim even to any such position will have to be carefully considered.

We must bear in mind throughout our consideration that it is not a question of *The* State, a single unique entity existing alone in a circumambient void, but of ' States ' existing in many different communities at different stages of development, and entering into the most varied relationships one with another.   When we speak of ' the State,' therefore, we are only using a class-name to which we can attach our generalisations as predicates. We are ignoring non-essential differences between one State and another, and concentrating on those essential characteristics which States have in common.

This, however, is to give too inclusive and generalised a scope to our treatment of the subject. Although we shall sometimes be referring to characteristics common to all States at all times and stages of development, we shall be using in the main for purposes of illustration 'the modern State,' that is, the States which exist in our own time and stage of civilisation. Taking the nature common to these States as our basis, we shall attempt to arrive, from the study of their common nature, at some conception of their true function in the Society of to-day and to-morrow. Further than that we can hardly hope to go ; for a new generation and a new degree of social development will inevitably call for a restatement of social theory.

Let us begin with a brief summary and analysis of the principal activities of the modern State, that is, of the States which exist in civilised communities in the world of to-day. Here, again, it would, of course, be useful to attempt a complete and exhaustive enumeration. Nor is it necessary to our purpose, which is only that of securing sufficient material to work upon in our attempt to discover the State's function in the Society of to-day. As we saw in our discussion of the principle of function, it is far from being the case that every actual activity of the State forms a part of its social function ; but it is the case that the function of the State can only be sought among activities which the State does, in some degree, already exercise. In order to discover the function of the State, it is therefore necessary to adopt a double procedure. We have first to examine, and select from, the actual activities of the State those which are, *prima facie*, essential, and we have then to examine the fundamental nature and constitution of the State with a view to determining which of these essential activities can be regarded as belonging to its function.

It is a commonplace observation that during the last two generations at least the activities of the State have been undergoing constant and rapid multiplication and expansion. Moreover, it is generally recognised that this expansion has been far more extensive in the economic, than in any other sphere. When Locke wrote his *Treatises on Civil Government*, interpreting in them the ideas and social situation of the English Revolution of 1688-9, it was still easy to regard the function of the State as strictly specific and limited, because its actual activities were in the main specific and limited, and were in process of actual construction. To-day, whatever may be the true function of the State, there is an undeniable temptation to conclude, on the basis of its actual activities, that its functions are practically universal and unlimited. Such a conclusion, whether it be right or wrong, at least goes with the grain of present-day Society. Yet it may be that Locke was nearer to being right than those social theorists who are ready to conclude, because the State does everything in fact, that its social function is pantopragmatic and universal.

To-day, almost every developed State is ceaselessly active in economic affairs. It passes Factory Acts, and other legislation designed to ensure a minimum of protection to the workers engaged in production : it regulates wages and hours : it attempts to provide for and against unemployment : it intervenes, successfully or unsuccessfully, in industrial disputes : it compels employers to provide compensation for accidents, and both employers and workers to contribute to social insurance funds which it administers. On the other hand, it regulates to some extent the commercial operations of financiers and employers, restricts or pretends to restrict trusts and profiteering, uses its consular service and special agents to aid foreign trade, encourages, subsidises and assists in industrial research, enacts laws affecting, and enters into many formal and informal relationships with capitalist interests and associations. Moreover, more and more it embarks itself upon economic enterprises, conducts a Post Office or a railway service, and becomes the direct employer of vast numbers of its own citizens, incidentally often imposing political and other disqualifications upon them on the ground that they are State employees.

To all this industrial and commercial activity of the national State must be added the no less complex activities of local authorities acting under the laws enacted by the State—municipal and other local bye-laws regulating industry and commerce, and the extending operations of ' municipal trading.' It will, however, be more convenient to consider the character and activities of local authorities separately at a later stage, although no clear or hard and fast line can be drawn between a State and a local authority in those cases where ' federal,'

THE STATE

'Dominion' or even 'regionalist' forms of government exist.

There is a further economic activity of the State which is more and more becoming manifest in our own day. Taxation is, in its origin, merely a method of collecting from individuals that proportion of their incomes which must be diverted from their personal use to meet the necessary expenses of State administration. But, as the activities of the State expand, taxation shows a marked tendency to become also a method of redistributing incomes within the community. This new tendency emerges already in systems of graduated taxation; but it becomes the leading principle in those proposals, nowhere yet carried far into effect, which aim at its definite and deliberate use as a means to at least comparative equality of income.[1]

Apart from taxation for administrative purposes, the present economic activities of the State are largely of recent growth. This is not to say that the State had not previously engaged in economic action on a large scale, as for instance under what is known as the 'Mercantile System.' But between the 'Mercantile System' and the economic activity of the modern State intervenes in many cases a period of comparative inactivity—*laissez faire*—following upon the changes caused by the Industrial Revolution. In the Middle Ages, when economic activities were largely in the hands of the Guilds, and

[1] The State Bonus Scheme, actively advocated by Mr. Dennis Milner and his colleagues of the State Bonus League, is an advanced example of this tendency. It is a definite proposal for a redistribution by the State, on a basis of equality, of a considerable proportion of the communal income.

85

in the period of the Industrial Revolution, when they were largely in the hands of competitive capitalists, the State's intervention in economic matters was, comparatively, very restricted indeed.

Extensive as the economic activities of the State are, it will be agreed that they have not yet, in any actual State, reached an essentially central position. This might occur, and would probably occur if the pure Collectivists had their way; but, for the present, the central position is still occupied by political and co-ordinating rather than by economic activities, although the latter constantly threaten the position of the two former. Our next inquiry must be into the nature of the *political* activities of the State.

The word 'political' is one round which a high degree of ambiguity has gathered. It has very various associations, with the Πόλις, or City-State, of the Greeks, with the modern Nation-State, with the whole complex of social action, with purely party and parliamentary activities, and so forth. Here I am using the word in a definite and specific sense. I mean by *political* activities those activities which are concerned with the social regulation of those personal relationships which arise directly out of the fact that men live together in communities, and which are susceptible to direct social organisation.[1]

In this, as in many other cases, it is easier and perhaps more illuminating, to illustrate than to define. What, we must ask, are the main types of actual political activity exercised by the State?

[1] See *ante*, p. 67, for *political* association.

THE STATE

Marriage is at once a civil and a religious institution. The State regulates the relations between individuals by enacting laws dealing with marriage and its dissolution, the care of children, the conduct arising out of sexual relationships in all their forms. It makes laws for the prevention and punishment of crime, for the care and treatment of lunatics, the feeble-minded and others who are not in a position to look after themselves. It is vitally concerned with many relationships quite apart from sex crime or abnormality, and constantly lays down rules of convenience and convention for the guidance of men in their mutual relationships. If it covers any considerable area or includes any large number of inhabitants, it must recognise or establish local authorities similar to itself but with more limited powers, and makes general rules for the guidance of these bodies in their various activities. In fact, it is concerned mainly with personal rights and the means of reconciling them, and with those limitations of personal conduct which are essential to the existence of a co-ordinated system of personal rights.

Where classes exist in the community, the State often exercises further political activity in sustaining, recognising, and modifying class privileges and class exclusions. It creates, say, a peerage, and from time to time elevates the latest exalted servant of the public, or newspaper proprietor, or *nouveau riche*, to membership of the peerage. It enacts special privileges for one class or another, or passes special legislature discriminating against a class. In the extreme case, its political activity assumes the form of a class dictatorship. This is the bad side of the State's political activity.

Thirdly, the State of to-day possesses increasingly important activities of *co-ordination*. It is largely concerned in adjusting the relations between association and association, or institution and institution, or institution and association, or between other associations or institutions and itself. It enacts laws regulating the form and scope of associative activity, friendly society law, law affecting banks, companies, partnerships, Trade Unions, clubs, associations of any and every sort. In some degree, it regulates all religious associations, and, in some countries, the existence of an Established Church considerably increases the extent of its religious intervention. There is one theory of the State which regards it as primarily a co-ordinating body, devoted not to any specific functions of its own, but to the co-ordinating of the various functional associations within Society.[1]

I do not claim that this summary of the activities of States is exhaustive or inclusive, nor do I desire to make it so. It can, with one further development, be made sufficient for our purpose. I have so far dealt almost entirely with the internal activities of ' the State,' and ignored its external relations, whether with other States, or with anything wholly or partly outside its geographical boundaries. I have done this because ' international ' or external activity cannot be regarded as a particular province of State activity, in the same sense as economic,

[1] This view has been often expressed in the columns of the *New Age*, over the signature ' National Guildsmen.'

political and co-ordinating activities. International action arises in relation to each of these provinces of State activity, and has, besides, special problems of its own. Thus the State takes external economic action in the development of foreign trade, external political action in connexion, say, with international provisions regarding crime, marriage, naturalisation, and other questions of personal status and convenience which involve a measure of activity transcending State boundaries. In its activity of co-ordination, it is confronted with the problem of international association, from the Roman Catholic Church to the Socialist International.

These forms of external State action may either lead to quarrels and disagreements between States, or they may bind States together and lead towards a sort of super-State, or at least Society or League of States bound together for the performance of specific functions or the exercise of specific activities. Hitherto, the external actions of States have been far more fertile in disagreement than in organised co-operation ; but it does not follow that this will always be the case. Indeed, a proper understanding and adjustment of the internal functions of the State will be likely to exercise a profound and beneficent action upon its relations with other States, and to set it upon the road of organised international co-operation which other forms of association are more forward in following than the State has been in the past. .

A full discussion of the external aspects of State action, however, would be foreign to our present purpose, which is in the main that of disentangling the true functions of the State from the network of its present activities. By what test can we so test these activities as to make the real nature and function of the State stand out from among them clear and well-defined ? The first step in applying our test must be to investigate the State from a different point of view, to regard it in the light, not of its activities, but of its structure and composition. We may then hope, by bringing its activities into relation to its structure, to discover its function in the complex of organised Society.

How, then, is the State composed ? And what is its structural principle ? These are not easy questions to answer, because any attempt to answer them is likely to open at once large controversial questions. Moreover, the structure of different States, or of the same State at different times, appears to be essentially different. What is there in common between the structure of a pure despotism, in which a monarch is supposed to possess absolute and unlimited power, and a State in which all power rests, at any rate in theory, upon the consent and active co-operation of the whole body of the people ?

It must be noted that the activities of a ' despotic ' and of a ' democratic ' State may be identical, while their structural principles seem to be vitally different. But are their structural principles as fundamentally different as they seem ? Every despotism which seeks at all to justify its existence seeks to do so on one or another of three principles. Either it claims to be based upon ' divine right and appointment ' of the ruler, or it

THE STATE

claims to be acting in the interests of the ruled, and therefore in conformity with their real will, or it claims to be based upon the actual consent of the ruled, tacit or expressed. With despotisms which do not seek to justify their existence we are not concerned, since in them it is manifest that social obligation, on which the possibility of a coherent Society depends, is not present.

We are left, then, with three possible justifications of despotism, and it must be admitted that all three finally reduce themselves to a common form—the consent, in one form or another, of the ruled. This is clear in the third form of the theory of despotism, which is based on actual consent. In the second form, the consent is not actual, but unless it is real the justification fails. It depends upon the metaphysical conception of the ' real will,' different from the actual will and willing always the good. It claims, in fact, to be the consent of the ' better selves ' of the ruled. The third theory, that of divine right, seems at first sight to have nothing to do with human consent ; but if God has willed that a man shall be king, it is clear that the ' better selves ' of all men have willed this too, and that, if divine right is established, universal consent ought to follow as a matter of course.

Any attempt to justify a despotic State therefore brings us back to the same principle as that on which ' democratic ' States are usually justified— the consent of the ruled. It is true that in a despotism this consent cannot, unless the despotic is elected, pass beyond acquiescence, whereas in democracy consent may become, and in real democracy must become, active co-operation. Still, a common ground of principle has been established, and the State, whatever its form of power, is seen to rest on the consent of those who are its citizens, subjects, members or human constituents.

If once the principle of consent is established as the basis of the State, it is impossible to set limits to the operation of the principle. If the members consent to despotism, well and good ; but as soon as they desire to assume a more active co-operation in the affairs of State, they have clearly a right to do so. The fullest democracy in action is only the logical development of the principle of consent, expanded by the application of actual human wills —that is, of the will to self-government. If this is so, we can safely take the ' democratic State ' as the developed form of ' *the* State,' and expect, in laying bare its structure, to lay bare the structure of States in general.

The only obstacle in the way of our immediately adopting this course is the metaphysical doctrine of the real ' will '—a doctrine which we shall again and again encounter as an influence obscuring our attempt to study the character of social organisation. If the doctrine of a real will different from anybody's actual will is accepted, all arguments for democracy, that is government by the actual wills of the ruled, go by the board. But so equally do all arguments for everything else ; for we are left without means of ascertaining the nature or content of this real will. The content of actual wills we can know up to a point : the content of the real

THE STATE

will we cannot know at all. We can only know what we believe to be good, and thereupon, by a quite gratuitous assumption, assume our conception of the good to be the content of everybody's real will. Or, if we are not quite sure ourselves that we know all the good, we can stand back astonished at the magnitude of the State and its works, and say that anything so big must be good. Many idealist social theorists have virtually done this, and made of the doctrine of the real will, in its application to social theory, no more than a colossally fraudulent justification of ' things as they are.' [1]

I shall content myself with leaping rather lightly over this metaphysical obstacle, referring my readers to the book of Professor Hobhouse, and reserving the matter for fuller treatment at a later stage. I shall assume, then, that actual wills are real wills, or at least near enough to reality to be going on with, and I shall therefore assume that the basis of the State's structure is to be found in the actual consent of its members.

But here we encounter our first real difficulty. Who are the *members* of the State, and, indeed, can the State be said to have any members ? I am using the word ' members ' because it is the most neutral word I can find. We usually speak of ' citizens ' or ' subjects ' ; but one of these words has about it the implication of despotism and the other that of the actual exercise of political rights.

[1] For an excellent onslaught upon some such theories, see *The Metaphysical Theory of the State*, by L. T. Hobhouse. For an awful example of them, see the writings of Dr. Bernard Bosanquet.

I therefore avoid them for the present, because I want to avoid equally for the present both these implications.

The State, as an association, has members, and its members are all the persons ordinarily resident within the area within which the State ordinarily exercises authority. Such persons are members of the State, whether or not they have votes or other political privileges, by virtue merely of their ordinary residence within the State area. For the State is, for the dwellers within its area, a compulsory association, and its compulsory character is revealed in two ways—in its power to compel all persons in its area, and in the right of all such persons to membership of it. When we say that the State rests upon consent, we mean that it rests upon the consent of an effective proportion of *all* the dwellers within its area.

Membership of the State is, however, an almost barren theory without recognised political rights—for without such rights a member can only make his voice heard in time of revolution, when the ordinary procedure of the State is in abeyance. What right, we must ask, does membership of the State give to the recognition of actual political rights? The answer is partly implied in what we have said already of consent as the basis of the State. The members of the State have the right to translate a passive consent into an active co-operation by the assumption of political rights. This they habitually do by gradually extending the franchise and other political rights to new sections of the population, as these sections become articulate

94

in advancing their claim. The logical completion of this development is universal suffrage as the expression of a political articulateness generally diffused through all sections of the people.

I shall take, then, as the basis of examination of the structure of the State, a State possessing the institution of universal suffrage. What is the structural principle of such a State ? Regarded as a whole, it is a compulsory association including all the dwellers within a particular area. Its basis is therefore territorial and inclusive, whereas the basis of a Trade Union is vocational and selective. The essence of the State is to include all sorts of people, without reference to the sort of people they are, the sort of beliefs they hold, or the sort of work they do.

I do not mean, of course, that there is not usually a very important element of identity of character, way of life, and even occupation, among the members of a particular State. This element of identity is strongest in the City-State, and very strong in the State whose area is the area of a Nation. But it is not the essential principle of the State form of grouping. There are States which are not coterminous with Nations, and State and Nation are essentially different things. A Nation may be a community, but it cannot be, though it may possess, a State. A Nation is not an association ; a State is.

The State, then, is an inclusive territorial association, ignoring differences between men and compulsorily taking in every one who ordinarily dwells within its area. This being its principle, how can we discover its function ? The answer will be found by asking and answering a further question.

Why does the State ignore the differences between men and include all sorts and conditions, and what is the sphere of action, or social function, marked out for it by the adoption of this structure ? It ignores the differences between men because it is concerned not with their differences, but with their identity, and its function and interest are concerned with men's identity and not with their differences. Objectively stated, this principle takes the following form. The concern of the State, as an association including all sorts and conditions of men, is with those things which concern all sorts and conditions of men, and concern them, broadly speaking, in the same way, that is, in relation to their identity and not to their points of difference.

The State exists primarily to deal with those things which affect all its members more or less equally and in the same way. Let us try to see clearly what are the effects of this principle. It excludes from the primary functions of the State— from its social function *par excellence*—those spheres of social action which affect different members of it in different degrees and in various ways. This does not mean that the State must not concern itself with any such spheres of action, but only that they do not form part of its primary function, and may fall within the functions of other forms of association. We are not concerned as yet so much with limiting the province of the State as with discovering what is its undisputed and peculiar sphere of activity.

THE STATE

Let us look back now to the point from which we set out—to our brief account of the existing activities of the State. Which of these activities clearly correspond to the definition we have just given, and are, by their correspondence, clearly marked out as essential activities of the State. We divided the actual activities of the State into three main divisions —economic, political and co-ordinative. Let us first look at each of these three divisions in general and as a whole, proceeding to a further analysis of them as we find it to be required.

Economic activities for the most part clearly affect the various members of the community [1] in different degrees and in various ways. For it is here that one of the most easily recognisable and organisable differences between man and man comes into play. Coal mining affects the coal miner in quite a different way from that in which it affects the rest of the people, and so through the whole list of trades and vocations. Of course, coal mining does affect not only the miner, but also everybody else ; but the point is that it affects the miner in a different manner and degree.

Here, however, a difficulty at once arises. Each trade or vocation affects those who follow it in a different way and degree from the way and degree in which it affects others ; but many vital industries and services do also, from another point of view, affect almost everybody in very much the same way.

---

[1] I use the terms ' members of the community ' and ' members of the State ' indifferently, assuming that the geographical area of the community coincides with that of the State. The argument is not affected.

AN INTRODUCTION TO SOCIAL THEORY

We must all eat and drink, be clothed, housed and warmed, be tended in sickness and educated in childhood and youth, and our common needs in these and other respects give rise to a common relation, that of consumers or users of the products and service rendered by those who follow the various trades and vocations concerned.

It is upon the fact that the Collectivist theory of the State is based. The Collectivists, or State Socialists, regard the State as an association of consumers, and claim for it supremacy in the economic sphere on the ground that consumption, at least in relation to the vital industries and services, is a matter that concerns everybody equally and in the same way. This, however, is to ignore a difference as vital as the identity on which stress is laid. The most that can be claimed for the State in the economic sphere on account of the identical interest of all the members of the community in consumption is State control of consumption, and not State control of production, in which the interests of different members of the community are vitally different.

The economic sphere thus falls at once into two separable parts—production and consumption, in one of which all interests tend to be identical, while in the other, production, they tend to be different. Consumption is thus marked off as falling, *prima facie*, within the sphere of the State, while production is no less clearly marked off as falling outside it.

We shall have to pursue this question further at a later stage, when we examine directly the economic structure of Society. There is, however, one question, arising immediately out of this distinction, with which we must deal at the present stage. We saw in our summary of State activities that taxation tends to become, and to be regarded as, not merely a means of raising revenue for public purposes, but a means of redistributing the national income. May not this tendency provide the key to the State's function in relation to consumption? If there is one thing in the economic sphere which affects everybody equally and in the same way it is the question of income, on which the nominal amount of consumption depends. Closely bound up with this is the question of price, which, in its relation to income, determines the real amount of consumption. Income and prices, then, seem to fall clearly within the province of the State, and the determination of them forms an integral part of the State's functions.

The State, then, regulates consumption primarily through income and prices. By these means it acts upon the general level and distribution of consumption, and not directly upon the consumption of any particular commodity. It is, however, clear that, in the case of many staple commodities and vital services, not only the general level of consuming power, but also the consumption and supply of a particular commodity or service, affects everybody more or less equally and in the same way. Of course, there are many other commodities whose consumption affects only a part of the people, or affects different sections in very unequal measure. In such cases the State has no primary function. Having regulated the general distribution of consuming power, it can leave to *ad hoc* bodies the expression of the consumers' point of view in relation to such commodities or services.

But in the case of the vital commodities and services which, broadly speaking, affect everybody equally and in the same way, there is a *prima facie* argument for State regulation, and it is clear that regulation must be done either by the State or by some body or bodies reproducing its structure and similarly based upon general suffrage and an inclusive and non-selective electorate. The question whether the State or some other body or bodies so constituted should assume these functions depends upon the degree in which the combined performance of political functions and of these specialised economic functions can be undertaken with satisfactory results by the same group of elected persons, or whether it is necessary that the same body of electors should choose different persons and representative bodies for the performance of functions so essentially different and calling for such different capacities and acquirements.[1]

The *political* activities of the State give rise to no such complex problems as its economic activities. Here the only question that arises in most cases is whether a particular sphere of personal relationship ought to be regulated or left unregulated. If it is to be regulated at all, it falls clearly according to our principle within the proper sphere of the State. For in personal relationship, whether

---

[1] This point is more fully developed in Chapter VI., where it is urged that if a person is chosen to ' represent ' a body of electors, he can only be a real representative if his function is clearly and specifically limited and defined. See also *Introduction to Self-Government in Industry* (edition of 1919).

THE STATE

regulation is based on moral principles or on principles of convenience, the regulation clearly affects, or should affect, and would but for class and economic distinctions affect, every one equally and in the same way. ' Political ' activities, then, in the sense which we have given to the phrase, belong clearly to the function of the State.

What, then, of activities of *co-ordination*, such as we described earlier in this chapter ? Here a far greater difficulty arises. To entrust the State with the function of co-ordination would be to entrust it, in many cases, with the task of arbitrating between itself and some other functional association, say, a Church or a Trade Union. But just as no man ought to be the judge of his own case, so ought no association. Therefore, co-ordination cannot belong to the function of the State ; but neither can it belong to that of any other functional association.

We should reach the same conclusion if we ignored the argument against making the State judge in its own cause, and attended only to the nature of co-ordinating activities. For such activities clearly bring in many questions which do not affect everybody equally and in the same way, but affect various groups in essential different ways. Therefore, once more, we must conclude that the function of co-ordination does not belong to the State.

This is a conclusion of far-reaching and fundamental importance ; for if the State is not the co-ordinating authority within ' the community, neither is it, in the sense usually attached to the

term, 'sovereign.' But the claim to ' Sovereignty '
is that on which the most exalted pretensions of the
State are based. Almost all modern theories of
the State attribute to it not merely a superiority
to all other forms of association, but an absolute
difference in kind, by virtue of which it is supposed
to possess, in theory at least, an unlimited authority
over every other association and over every
individual in the community.

If our account of the nature of the State is correct,
its functions must be newly defined and limited in
terms of its specific functions, and with this definition and limitation its claim to Sovereignty falls
utterly to the ground. We cannot, however, so
lightly destroy an almost universally held theoretical
position, and, in order to make perfectly plain our
reasons for denying it, we must at once embark on
a discussion of the closely related questions of
democracy and representation. We can then
return to our study of the State with a better hope
of making the argument perfectly clear.

CHAPTER VI

DEMOCRACY AND REPRESENTATION

THERE is in our own day an almost general prejudice in favour of democracy. Almost everybody is a 'democrat,' and the name of democracy is invoked in support of the most diverse social systems and theories. This general acceptance of the name of democracy, even by persons who are obviously not in any real sense 'democrats,' is perhaps largely to be explained by the fact that the idea of democracy has become almost inextricably tangled up with the idea of representative government, or rather with a particular theory of representative government based on a totally false theory of representation.

This false theory is that one man can 'represent' another or a number of others, and that his will can be treated as the democratic expression of their wills. Stated in this form, the theory admits of only one answer. No man can represent another man, and no man's will can be treated as a substitute for, or representative of, the wills of others.

This may look, at first sight, like a complete denial of every form of representative government, and an affirmation of the futility of all elections.

It is, however, nothing of the sort ; it is not an attack upon, or an attempt to destroy the theoretic basis of, representative government, but an attempt to restate the theory of representation in a truer form. In order that it may be fully understood, we must bring it into relation to the doctrine of function expounded in previous chapters. We have seen that, just as every action of an individual aims at some specific object, so men form and enter associations in pursuit of specific objects which can be best pursued in common by or through an organised group. Every association, then, has a specific object or objects, and it is in pursuit of some or all of these objects that men consent to be members of the association.

Every association which sets before itself any object that is of more than the most rudimentary simplicity finds itself compelled to assign tasks and duties, and with these powers and a share of authority, to some of its members in order that the common object may be effectively pursued. It elects, perhaps, a Secretary, a President, a Treasurer and an Executive Committee, and empowers these persons to act on behalf of the association in certain definite ways and within certain limits. In the smaller and more localised associations, much of the control of the proceedings of the association may remain in the hands of the general body of the members ; but as soon as it becomes too large or too dispersed for a general meeting to transact business, or if the members are too preoccupied with other affairs to make it their constant concern, the detailed regulation of its proceedings passes largely into the hands of a comparatively small number of its members, officers, committee men, delegates or representatives. In the largest and most complex forms of association, such as the State, the ordinary member is reduced to a mere voter, and all the direction of actual affairs is done by representatives —or misrepresentatives.

At the best, representative government gives rise to many inconveniences, to what Walt Whitman described as " the never-ending audacity of elected persons," and Rousseau as " the tendency of all government to deteriorate." With these inconveniences we shall have to deal at a later stage ; but here we are concerned only to make clear the nature of the representative relation as it exists in such associations as we have spoken of above.

In the majority of associations, the nature of the relation is clear enough. The elected person— official, committee man, or delegate—makes no pretension of substituting his personality for those of his constituents, or of representing them except in relation to a quite narrow and clearly defined purpose or group of purposes which the association exists to fulfil. There is, then, in these cases, no question of one man taking the place of many ; for what the representative professes to represent is not the whole will and personalities of his consti-tuents, but merely so much of them as they have put into the association, and as is concerned with the purposes which the association exists to fulfil.

This is the character of all true representation. It is impossible to represent human beings as selves or centres of consciousness ; it is quite possible to represent, though with an inevitable element of distortion which must always be recognised, so much of human beings as they themselves put into associated effort for a specific purpose.

True representation, therefore, like true association, is always specific and functional, and never general and inclusive. What is represented is never man, the individual, but always certain purposes common to groups of individuals. That theory of representative government which is based upon the idea that individuals can be represented as wholes is a false theory, and destruction of personal rights and social well-being.

The fact that a man cannot be represented as a man seems so obvious that it is difficult to understand how many theories of government and democracy have come to be built upon it. Each man is a centre of consciousness and reason, a will possessed of the power of self-determination, an ultimate reality. How can one such will be made to stand in place of many? How can one man, being himself, be at the same time a number of other people? It would be a miracle if he could; but it is a risky experiment to base our social system upon a hypothetical miracle.

Functional representation is open to no such objection. It does not lay claim to any miraculous quality: it does not profess to be able to substitute the will of one man for the wills of many. Its adherents recognise the element of distortion which exists in all representation; but to them this distortion is not a problem, but an inevitable fact. It does not annihilate or detract from the will of any individual; it merely provides a basis whereby, when the individual has made up his mind that a certain object is desirable, he can co-operate with his fellows in taking the course of action necessary for its attainment.

Of course, I do not intend to convey the idea that there are just so many functions in Society, and that to each corresponds exactly its own functional association and form of representation. The need of Society for functional association and representation expands and develops as Society becomes larger and more complex. A special form of association and representation, at one time unnecessary, may become necessary as the work of Society increases in a particular direction. Moreover, in a very small Society, such as the ancient City-State, where the direct participation of the mass of the people in government was possible, functional association was only needed in a very limited degree, and it was often possible for the people to choose directly their functional representatives without any intervening stage of functional association. The principle of representation, however, is the same; the representative represents not persons, but definite and particular purposes common to a number of persons.

Having made plain our conception of the true nature of representation, we can now look more closely at its consequences. In proportion as the purposes for which the representative is chosen lose clarity and definiteness, representation passes into misrepresentation, and the representative character of the acts resulting from association disappears.

Thus, misrepresentation is seen at its worst to-day in that professedly omnicompetent ' representative ' body—Parliament—and in the Cabinet which is supposed to depend upon it. Parliament professes to represent all the citizens in all things, and therefore as a rule represents none of them in anything. It is chosen to deal with anything that may turn up, quite irrespective of the fact that the different things that do turn up require different types of persons to deal with them. It is therefore peculiarly subject to corrupt, and especially to plutocratic, influences, and does everything badly, because it is not chosen to do any definite thing well. This is not the fault of the actual Members of Parliament ; they muddle because they are set the impossible task of being good at everything, and representing everybody in relation to every purpose.

There can be only one escape from the futility of our present methods of parliamentary government ; and that is to find an association and method of representation for each function, and a function for each association and body of representatives. In other words, real democracy is to be found, not in a single omnicompetent representative assembly, but in a system of co-ordinated functional representative bodies.

There is another, and a simpler, line of argument which leads straight to the same conclusion as we have already reached. It is obvious that different people are interested in, and good at doing, different things. It is therefore equally obvious that, if I am a sensible person, I shall desire to choose different people to represent my wishes in relation to different things. To ask me to choose one man to represent me in relation to everything is to insult my intelligence, and to offer me every inducement to choose some one so colourless that he is unlikely to do anything at all—because he will at least probably do no great harm, and no great notice will be taken of him. This is how parliamentary elections usually work out at the present time.

But, if I am asked to choose a different person to represent my wishes in relation to each of the main groups of social purposes of which I am conscious, I shall do my best to choose in each case the man who is most fitted to represent my views and to carry them into effect. In short, the one method will inevitably result in government by the incompetent ; the other will at least give every chance for competent representatives to be chosen.

Democracy, then, must be conceived in the first place as a co-ordinated system of functional representation. But, as soon as we introduce the word ' democracy,' we raise a further question, that of the relation between me and my functional representative after I have chosen him. In fact, we find ourselves in the thick of the old controversy of ' representative versus delegate.'

Does our revised theory of representation throw any light upon this controversy ? Or, in other words, is the question whether the elected person, once he has been elected, should follow his own will or should be instructed as far as possible on every issue by those who have chosen him, to be answered in a different way when the theory of representation is different ? I think the theory of representation which we adopt must make a considerable difference to our view of the relation of the elected person to his constituents.

In the first place, attempts to make the elected person a mere delegate must always break down, whatever the form of representation. There are many issues on which it is not merely undesirable, but impossible, to tie down a delegate by instructions, because unforeseen situations and complications constantly arise. If for no other reason, pure delegation must break down because the delegate is so often waiting for further instructions that nothing gets done, and the best opportunities for action are continually being missed. On the other hand, pure 'representation' without instructions or counsel from the electors approaches very nearly to false representation, substituting, even within a restricted sphere, the will of one for the wills of many.

Our functional democracy, based on functional associations and representations, provides a way out of this difficulty. It enables us to combine representation with constant counsel from the constituents, and thus makes it possible to abandon the theory of delegation without imperilling democratic control. The chief difficulty of democratic control over the representative in the political sphere to-day is that, as soon as the voters have exercised their votes, their existence as a group lapses until the time when a new election is required. No body or group remains in being to direct upon the elected person a constant stream of counsel and criticism. Consequently, the elected person must either receive full instructions at the time of election, which produces an intolerable situation as soon as there is any change in the circumstances, or else he must become a pure representative, acting on his own responsibility and consequently expressing only his own will and not those of his constituents. This dilemma exists wherever the body of electors does not remain in being and activity as a body throughout the tenure of office of the elected person.

Functional democracy, in which representatives emanate from functional associations which have a permanent being, meets this difficulty. It is no longer necessary for the group to instruct its representative, because it can continue throughout his time of office to criticise and advise him, and because, I would add, it can at any time recall him if it is not satisfied with the way in which he is doing his job. Recall is, in fact, the final safeguard, while criticism and advice are the normal means of keeping the representation democratic.

In our own day, experience of bad leaders, both in the State and in other forms of association, has bred an almost general distrust of leadership, and a strong desire, especially on the so-called ' left wing,' to do away with leaders, and substitute direct control by the ' rank and file' through delegates duly instructed how to act and vote. But there is no reason to take the badness of present-day leaders as a sign that the whole idea of leadership should be given up. Certainly, before we adopt any such drastic expedient, all the circumstances ought to be fully explored. But, at the very beginning of this explanation, the biggest single cause of the collapse of leadership is plainly to be seen. The absence of any true principle of representation in the sphere of the State, the failure that is to 'functionalise' the State, and to make the political representative a functional representative, is the main cause of the perversion of political leadership. But the perversion of political leadership is, in its turn, the main cause of the perversion of leadership elsewhere. The Trade Union leader, and many other 'functional' leaders, have their eyes fixed upon Parliament, and the thought of Parliament distracts them from their proper work. Moreover, this parliamentary *arrière-pensée* is an important factor in causing the wrong leaders to be selected, and the wrong candidates to offer themselves for selection.

We must preserve leadership without sacrificing democratic control. Leadership is as vital to a democracy as to an aristocracy or a monarchy. And it is as true in a democracy as anywhere else that the good leader must be given a great deal of rope.

In a functional democracy, where the elected person is a representative and not a delegate, and where he acts not as a rule upon instructions, but upon criticism and advice, I believe that the good leader will find ample scope, as soon as the distrust which is born of false democracy has had time to wear off. It is true that he will be liable to summary recall ; but who believes that, after the initial mistakes, this power would be too freely exercised ? The risks are all the other way : it is of a too long tenure of office by second-rate men that we should be afraid. Functional democracy will give the good leader his first real chance of leading by his merits, with an instructed and active body of constituents behind him. For it must be remembered that not only will the representative be chosen to do a job about which he knows something, but he will be chosen by persons who know something of it too. Truly a revolutionary proposal for a democrat to make !

But some one will object, if I have this respect for leaders why do I insist on the right of recall ? I do so, because I have even more respect for human wills and personalities, and because I feel that democracy implies far more than the passive consent of the mass of the people in government. Democracy implies active, and not merely passive, citizenship, and implies for everybody at least the opportunity to be an active citizen, not only of the State, but of every association with which his personality or circumstances cause him to be concerned.

Those who profess to find the bond of Society in the passive consent of the mass of the people fall between two stools. If the mass of the people are necessary to the justification of the social order, they are necessary in the active and not in the passive mood. In other words, if we base our social theory upon the attitude of the mass of the people, we are logically driven to insist that this attitude ought to be as explicit and positive as possible.

A well-organised Society is one in which not merely is the administration good, but the wills of the members of the community are active, and find expresssion through the various associations and institutions of which Society is made up. It should be the aim of those who strive to direct the course of social organisation to promote the fullest participation of everybody in the work of government. This alone is true democracy, and this can only be secured by the fullest development of functional organisation. The current theory of representative government is a denial of this principle ; for, having chosen his representative, the ordinary man has, according to that theory, nothing left to do except to let other people govern him. Functional organisation and representation, on the other hand, imply the constant participation of the ordinary man in the conduct of those parts of the structure of Society with which he is directly concerned, and which he has therefore the best chance of understanding. A man may be pardoned for not quite knowing for whom to vote in a parliamentary election, or how to appraise the career of his Member of Parliament, because the Member of Parliament of to-day is elected not for any clearly defined purpose, but in the void, to deal with anything that may chance to turn up. A functional association, on the other hand, is concerned with doing a definite job, and its officers are also concerned with getting that definite job done. The member is connected with the association because its business is his business, and he is therefore able far more intelligently to initiate and criticise action in relation to it than in relation to an *omnium gatherum* miscalled ' politics.' Functional organisation gives every one the chance of being, in the measure of his competence and interest, an active citizen.

This does not mean that, in a functional democracy, each person will count for one and no person for more than one. That is the cant of false democracy. The essence of functional democracy is that a man should count as many times over as there are functions in which he is interested. To count once is to count about nothing in particular : what men want is to count on the particular issues in which they are interested. Instead of ' One man, one vote,' we must say ' One man as many votes as interests, but only one vote in relation to each interest.'

This restatement of a democratic principle still leaves intact the equal voting power of unequal persons voting on a particular issue. That, too, is democracy, not because equalisation of votes can make unequal persons equal, but because the right way for the better man to ' pull his weight ' is not by casting more votes himself, but by influencing others to vote aright. Democracy involves leadership by influence.

Before we end this chapter, we must face a very foolish, but very often urged, objection to the whole idea of functional representation. Functional representation, we are told, is impossible because, in order to make it work, everybody will have to vote so many times over. I fail to see where the objection arises. If a man is not interested enough to vote, and cannot be roused to interest enough to make him vote, on, say, a dozen distinct subjects, he waives his right to vote, and the result is no less democratic than if he voted blindly and without interest. It is true that the result is not so democratic as it would be if everybody voted with interest and knowledge, but it is far more democratic than it would be if everybody voted without interest or knowledge, as they tend to do in parliamentary elections. Many and keen voters are best of all ; but few and keen voters are next best. A vast and uninstructed electorate voting on a general and undefined issue is the worst of all. Yet that is what we call democracy to-day.

CHAPTER VII

GOVERNMENT AND LEGISLATION

WE have seen that, as soon as any association passes beyond the doing of the most simple and elementary acts, it becomes necessary for it to have representatives—persons endowed with the right, within certain limits, to speak and act in the name of the association, to deliberate on its behalf, and to take the steps necessary for carrying out its decisions. The character and complexity of the representative methods adopted varies both with the size and geographical dispersion of the association, and with the complexity of the functions which it exists to perform. Thus, as long as it is possible for all the members to meet together and discuss each issue of policy as it arises, representatives, where they are required, will be unlikely to acquire any very great power, and will be mainly engaged in doing the routine work necessary to carry out the decisions of the general meeting. This is the position to-day in those parishes which are governed by a Parish Meeting, or in a small local Trade Union or other association.

At this stage, it will be seen, there may be rudimentary officials, permanent or occasional, corresponding to the fully developed executive officers of more advanced forms of association : there may be a committee, permanent or occasional, and also of an executive character. But there is as yet no representative legislative assembly, no body of men selected from the association, and legislating or laying down the main lines of policy in the name of all the members. This is a further development, which arises when it becomes impossible or inconvenient for all the members to meet and deliberate together. It is at this stage that the real problem of government arises, and the association creates for itself a representative assembly, entrusted with the task of legislation.

This does not mean that the final decision on questions of policy passes altogether and necessarily away from the whole body of the members. There remain two ways in which the whole of the members may still keep important decisions in their own hands. They may choose to act through delegates rather than representatives, and, although they cannot all meet together, the local members may hold meetings in a number of centres to instruct their delegate, or, in the alternative, to advise their representative, how to vote. Or they may adopt the institution of the referendum, and insist that important issues shall be submitted to a ballot vote of all the members.

Both these expedients, however, are extremely clumsy, when it is attempted to apply them to any but the broadest and simplest issues. For, in either case, every question has to be reduced to a simple

GOVERNMENT AND LEGISLATION

Aye or No, and the possibility of adjustments, amendments and new situations has to be left out of account. The method of referendum or instruction is, I believe, the right method where the broadest and simplest issues are concerned ; but it offers no help in dealing with the more complex and detailed issues which are constantly arising in almost every association.

Men are driven, therefore, to the expedient of the representative [1] legislative assembly for getting the ordinary day-to-day work of the more complex associations efficiently accomplished. In the less complex associations, very often no separate legislative assembly is created, but the Executive Committee acts also as a legislature within the limits which the purposes of the assembly require. The more complex type of association, however, usually creates a separate body for the task of legislation, and calls this body together as required, the Executive Committee remaining in being to carry out its decisions. In the most complex types of association, such as the State, the legislative assembly, as well as the Executive Committee, tends to become permanent and to remain in almost continuous session. Even Parliament, however, has only very gradually developed this permanent and continuous character. The early Parliaments were occasional bodies.

The purpose of this chapter is to investigate more

---

[1] It is necessary to bear in mind, throughout this chapter, the sense attached to the word ' representation.' It is always functional representation alone that is to be regarded as true representation.

closely than we have yet done the actual ways of operation of representative bodies and persons, in order to see how the will of the members finds expression through their representatives, and also how it is sometimes perverted and twisted in passing through the representatives' intermediary. One of the most illuminating chapters of Rousseau's *Social Contract* [1] deals with the ' tendency of government to deteriorate.' All action through representatives, he explains, involves to a certain extent the substitution of the wills of the representatives for those of the represented. Moreover, all groups of men, by experience of acting together, tend to develop in some degree a ' common will ' of their own. Chosen to express the ' common will ' of those whom they represent, they acquire a ' common will ' of their own different from that of the represented.

We have given in the last chapter our reasons for supposing that the definite limits and purposes of functional representatives make these dangers far less applicable to it than to so-called ' representation ' which is general and not functional. This, however, does not mean that, even with functional representation, the danger altogether disappears. It is, indeed, impossible that it should ever disappear, unless as the result of a miracle which would be also an overwhelming calamity. For the possibility of Society is based on the fact that, by acting together, men do as a rule develop an increasing sense of community. This is the very basis of Society ; but it has inevitably its bad, as

[1] *Social Contract*, bk. iii., chap. x.

well as its good, side. For it means that there is a sense of community among thieves as well as among honest men, and among members of committees and representative assemblies as well as among members of groups and associations. It means that, however faithfully the members of a committee may try to fulfil their whole duty to their members, an element of committee loyalty will almost inevitably enter into their actions. They will tend to back one another, whether they are right or wrong, and, when one of them is in danger of not being re-elected, the rest will often tend to support him even if they are aware that he is not the best man for the job. They will say one to another: "After all, we can't let down old Jones."

It is an easy and a highly popular pastime to gird at this idiosyncrasy of elected persons. But it is useless to abuse men for being clannish : we must rather recognise that the tendency to clannishness is the cement of the social system, and make up our minds to adopt the proper treatment in dealing with it. In the first place, we must always try to make the position of the representative as clear and definite as possible, clearly marking out his powers and functions and sphere of action and responsibility. And secondly, we must always try to provide as a background for the action of the representative, an active and continuously resourceful organised body of constituents. It is, I believe, the presence of this continuously active constituency that gives to the Soviet system, despite its countervailing disadvantages, its peculiar vitality. In short, it is for the body of the members to counteract the tendency to clannishness and even conspiracy on the part of the elected persons by being clannish and alert in pressing forward their own common wills.

I have so far spoken of the tendency of bodies of elected persons to substitute their own wills for the wills which they are supposed to represent as if it were a single and indivisible phenomenon. There is, however, an important distinction not so much in kind as in degree. There is the involuntary and often quite unconscious perversion or substitution which arises directly out of the fact that the members of the representative body are constantly acting and deliberating together; and there is also the conscious and voluntary perversion which may easily develop out of the unconscious perversion unless it is strongly checked by the presence of an active electorate. Cabinet Government is probably the worst instance of such deliberate and conscious perversion, of which the Party System is also an awful, but illuminating, example.[1] Any long continuance of this aggravated form of perversion proves that there is something seriously wrong either with the electorate as a whole or with the form of representation. Its constant presence in the political system of almost every country shows either that the peoples of the world are fundamentally corrupt or foolish, or that the generally accepted theory of representative government is radically wrong.

[1] See *The Party System*, by Hilaire Belloc and Cecil Chesterton, and *Democracy and the Organisation of Political Parties*, by Robert Michels.

GOVERNMENT AND LEGISLATION

Perversion, by the substitution of the will of the elected person for the wills he has been chosen to represent, is liable to occur in all types of representative body, and in all representative officials. We have therefore been able so far to treat representative institutions together without distinguishing for the most part between the various types. The next stage in our argument requires a more careful and detailed examination of the types of representative institutions with a view to ascertaining their right relationship one to another and to the represented. This brings us at once to a further discussion of the relation between legislative and executive power.

Many of the older writers on social science based the greater part of their exposition of the forms of social organisation upon the double distinction of legislative and executive power, or upon the triple distinction of legislature, executive and judiciary. I have endeavoured elsewhere to show that the distinction between legislature and executive provides no adequate basis for classifying the activities of modern Societies.[1] It may be possible to distinguish with clearness sufficient for all practical purposes between the work of law-making and the work of seeing to the execution of the laws (leaving aside for the moment the judicial aspect) as long as the social situations to be dealt with remain essentially simple and free from technical complications. But in the communities of to-day law-making and law-

---

[1] See *Self-Government in Industry*, chapter entitled ' The Nature of the State.' The final section of the same chapter deals with the judiciary.

administering inevitably run together. It is impossible to draft a law which will meet all the complexities of the case, and consequently our Parliaments and other legislative bodies are continually passing laws, many of whose clauses virtually delegate the power of legislation to the administrators, by providing that such and such matters may be dealt with by Order in Council or special order, or that the Minister concerned may make Orders and Regulations dealing with such and such a matter—provisions which effectively blur the already faint line of division between legislation and administration. In some cases, the legislative body attempts to retaliate and to establish a control over administration through parliamentary questions, interpellations, adjournment motions, votes to reduce a salary or a credit, Standing Committees, Select Committees and what not. The honours, however, under the parliamentary system, rest as a rule with the Executive, which steadily and successfully encroaches upon the sphere of legislation.

Nor are these phenomena confined to Cabinets and political assemblies. They appear also in other forms of association. Trade Union Executives try to seize the power of legislation out of the hands of Delegate Meetings ; and Delegate Meetings retaliate by encroaching upon the sphere of administration. Wherever much detailed and complicated business has to be transacted, the line of demarcation between legislature and executive tends to break down.

This breakdown has the more far-reaching consequences for social theory. Great stress used to be laid on the balance of powers between legislature and executive as a safeguard against tyranny and perversion. Whatever value this principle may have had in the past, it has little or none to-day, except as a minor safeguard within each particular association. Those who seek a balance of power in social organisation are therefore compelled to seek for a new principle of division. The old theory was an attempt to divide by *stages*—the law was first enacted by the legislature—and it then passed on to the succeeding stage of being administered by the executive. If this method of division by stages has broken down, there seems to be only one alternative open, if we desire to adhere to the principle of balance in any form. That alternative is to divide by *function*.

In earlier chapters of this book I have tried to establish the pre-eminence of function as the primary principle of social organisation. We have now to see what are the consequences of the acceptance of this principle in the sphere of government. Instead of a division based on the stage which an associative act has reached (the stage of law-making or the stage of administration), it gives us a new principle of division according, not to the stage, but to the *content* and purpose of the act. In other words, the principle of function implies that each functional form of association has and is its own legislature and its own executive.

This may seem either a very startling or a very commonplace proposition according to the manner in which it is interpreted. It is commonplace, if it only means that each association has to frame rules or laws for its own guidance, and to administer the rules or laws which it has made. It is startling, if it means that the laws of other functional associations have the same binding character and social status as the laws of the State.

Nevertheless, it is the startling form of the proposition which more nearly expresses what I mean. It flows as a necessary consequence from the denial of State Sovereignty and omnicompetence, and the affirmation of the functional character proper to the State, as to other associations, that the State's exclusive claim to the right of legislation goes by the board. It retains, of course, its right to legislate within its function ; but this right belongs also to other associations in relation to their numbers and within their respective functions.

This does not mean that all forms of functional legislation are equally important, any more than all forms of association are equally important. But it does mean that, in the measure of their importance, all forms of association acquire for their legislative acts a comparable social status.

The full implications of this functional division of legislation can only be made apparent at the end of the four following chapters. I must, however, at once try to meet, at least, provisionally, an objection which is almost certainly present already in the reader's mind. If the power of legislation is divided, he will ask, does not this also imply the division of coercive power ? Or, in other words, if the State's exclusive right to legislate is challenged, must not the State's exclusive right to use coercion be challenged also ?

I answer unhesitatingly that it must, and that

GOVERNMENT AND LEGISLATION

the State's monopoly of coercive power disappears with its loss of Sovereignty and of the monopoly of legislation. But, before we deal finally with the huge problem which is here raised, we must make quite certain that we know what we mean by coercion, and distinguish between various forms and uses of coercive power.

CHAPTER VIII

COERCION AND CO-ORDINATION

WE ended the last chapter with what was virtually an interrogation. What is the nature of coercive power in the community, and how, and in what forms, is it exercised?

Every association, by the mere fact of its existence, is endowed with some coercive power, and actually exercises some such power in the course of pursuing its object. This coercive power is not necessarily recognised by the community, and the courts of law sometimes disallow particular exercises of it by voluntary associations. Nevertheless it exists, and is freely exercised every day. Very many associations claim the right to fine their members for breach of the rules, and nearly all claim the final right of expelling a member who offends against the etiquette or rules of the association, or even who, in the opinion of the members, acts contrary to the interests of the association. Trade Unions and many other kinds of association constantly fine and often expel members, and it is very seldom that their right to do so is challenged by the courts in some particular case. Indeed, often the law of the State, so far from disallowing such associational coercion, backs it up and gives it legal sanction, or at least acquiesces in its decisions. This is especially the case in the ' self-governing ' professions, where the benchers of the Temple, or the Law Society, or the General Medical Council, freely use coercive power with the approval and sanction of the State. Thus, we can find ample instances of coercion by associations other than the State without inviting that great coercionist, spiritual and temporal, the Church.

There is, however, a distinction between three kinds of coercion which it is important to recognise at the outset. There is one kind of coercion which only affects a man's purse or property, that is coercion by fine. This is freely employed, not only by the State, but by most important types of association. There is a second kind of coercion which affects a man's freedom of action by limiting directly his range of opportunity and self-expression, as, for instance, by disfranchising him or forbidding him to work in a particular factory or occupation. The first is employed by the State and also by other forms of association ; the second occurs when the members of a Trade Union refuse to work with a non-Unionist, or expel a man from the Union and then refuse to work with him, or when an employers' association ' blacklists ' a man, and so prevents him from getting a job. ' Sending to Coventry ' is a less organised example of this kind of coercion.

The third form of coercion is that which directly affects a man's body, by limiting his right of movement, interning him, imprisoning him, or, in the last resort, hanging him, or shooting him, or cutting off his head. In civilised countries and in modern times these forms of diversion are usually, at least in the case of adults, the monopoly of the State. Civilisation, however, is often ready to resort to them without calling in the State in its dealings with what are politely called " non-adult " races, and also, in a less degree, in the case of children. The persistence of ' lynch law ' in some parts of the ' civilised ' world is an exception.

How are these forms of coercion related to the functional theory of Society which is propounded in this book ? Where, in other words, in a functionally organised Society, would the power of coercion in its various forms reside ?

It is clearly useless to deny all coercive power to any association which we are prepared to recognise at all as legitimate ; for whether we recognise the right to coercion or not, the power will remain and will be used. The most that is possible is to limit the forms of coercion which may be used by any particular functional association, and to reserve the right to the more stringent forms of coercion in the hands of that body which is most fit to exercise it. It is futile to endeavour to prevent an association which is allowed to make rules, and must make rules if it is to get its work done at all, from using some means to enforce their observance. Even if an association is deprived of the means of coercing its members directly, it will find indirect means of coercing them by placing obstacles in their way or withholding opportunities from them. Moreover, it is impossible altogether to prevent an association which exists to secure a particular object from coercing to a certain extent persons not its members who refuse to join it and pursue a contrary object or the same object in a different way. Here, again, the range and forms of coercion can be limited, but the possibility of coercion cannot be altogether abolished.

In a functionally organised Society, it seems reasonable to suppose that each functional association will employ directly the minor forms of coercion in relation to its own members, acting within strictly limited powers, and without the right to interfere with life or liberty of person. This, however, only drives us back upon a further question. What body in a functionally organised Society will define the limits within which coercion may be employed by the various associations, and itself exercise directly the major forms of coercion, if and when they are required ?

It is not difficult to recognise that this question brings us back to the very point at which we broke off in our discussion of the State.[1] We were there confronted with the question of the body which would, in a functional Society, exercise the powers of co-ordination at present claimed by the ' Sovereign State.' But clearly co-ordination and coercion go hand in hand.

We are now in a position to restate more clearly and fully the reasons which make it impossible to recognise the task of co-ordination as falling within the true function of the State. The claim on the State's behalf is usually based on the assumption that the State, because it represents and includes

[1] See Chapter V.

everybody within its area, is necessarily superior to other associations which only include some of the persons within its area.[1] But in what sense does the State represent and include everybody ? If our functional theory of representation is right, it may include everybody, but it does not include the whole of everybody ; it may represent some purposes common to everybody, but it does not represent all the purposes common to everybody. This being so, it can no longer lay claim to Sovereignty on the ground that it represents and includes everybody ; for the Sovereign, if there is one, must represent and include, as far as possible, the whole of everybody.

This it is impossible for any single association to-day, and indeed impossible for any complex of associations, to do completely. For there are vast tracts of life which are simply not susceptible to social organisation, and the purposes which they include are therefore not capable of being represented at all. This is, however, only a statement in other words of a fact which we have already recognised that, as the State is not co-extensive with organised Society, so Society is not co-extensive with community.

The principle of co-ordination which we are seeking cannot therefore be a principle co-ordinating all life within a given area, but only that part of life which is social and susceptible to social organisation. But it must co-ordinate the whole of that organisable social life. It cannot therefore be found in any

[1] The fact that they may also include persons outside the State's area is usually ignored.

COERCION AND CO-ORDINATION

one of the various forms of association which we have described ; for to each of these forms all the others are external, and no one of them could act as a co-ordinating agency either between the others or between itself and the rest. We are therefore reduced to the conclusion that no one among the many forms of functional association can be the co-ordinating body of which we are in search.

A dim perception of this difficulty has led social theorists into a variety of expedients. Some have maintained, like Rousseau, that Sovereignty resides inalienably in the whole body of the people and is incapable of being conferred upon any form of organisation at all. But such a view inevitably encounters the difficulty that, although the Sovereignty of the people is affirmed, no means can be found of making it actual, and all the important exercises of it pass into the hands of governing bodies which thus become virtually sovereign, even while their Sovereignty is being denied.[1]

Where this difficulty is recognised as being insuperable, at least in any large Society, the attempt is sometimes made to preserve popular Sovereignty by the constant use of the referendum. But a mere ' Yes or No ' vote, without the possibility of discussion or amendment, reduces popular Sovereignty to a farce except on the broadest issues, and once more the real power passes to the Government, or to whoever draws up the ballot papers and so decides the form of the question to be submitted. None of these mechanical expedients really gets over

[1] See my Introduction to Rousseau's *Social Contract* (*Everyman* edition), p. xxvi.

the difficulty. The referendum may be the best way of dealing with certain simple issues ; but by itself it certainly does not maintain popular Sovereignty ; nor does the addition of the initiative to it make any substantial difference.

If neither any single functional association nor the people itself can be the normal co-ordinating agency in a functionally organised Society, only one possibility remains. The co-ordinating body must be not any single association, but a combination of associations, a federal body in which some or all of the various functional associations are linked together.

It will be remembered that, in the chapter on " The Forms and Motives of Association," some attempt was made to discriminate between *essential* and *non-essential* forms of association. It was recognised that any such discrimination could be only approximate, because even the essential forms would tend to vary in different times and places. We did, however, succeed in establishing a working principle of discrimination. " The key to essentiality," we saw, " is the performance of some function which is vital to the coherent working of Society, and without which Society would be lopsided or incomplete." We saw there that, apart from religious association, which we reserved for special treatment, there are at least three forms of association which are to be regarded as generally essential. These are *political* association and the two forms of ' economic ' association or rather of association centring round the giving and receiving of services, that is to say, *vocational* and *appetitive* association.[1] We saw also that the essentiality of these forms of association in general does not suffice to establish the essentiality of any particular association belonging to one of these forms, unless two further conditions are satisfied. The motive which binds men together in the association must be a truly ' associative ' motive,[2] and the content or function of the particular association, and not merely of its form, must be important enough to warrant its being regarded as ' essential ' in accordance with the criterion stated above.

I do not propose to push further in this book the analysis of the essential forms and instances of association. To determine what actual associations are to be regarded as essential at a particular time and for a particular Society is a practical question, and is therefore alien to a work dealing with Social Theory.[3] Here we are concerned only with the general question—with the attempt to discover the principle of co-ordination in a functionally organised Society.

This principle has already been made inferentially clear. The co-ordinating agency can only be a combination, not of all associations, but of all essential associations, a Joint Council or Congress of the supreme bodies representing each of the main functions in Society. Each functional association will see to the execution of its own function, and for the co-ordination of the activities of the various

[1] See Chapter IV., pp. 63 ff.
[2] For the definition of ' associative ' motive, see pp. 34 ff.
[3] For a discussion on this point, see my *Self-Government in Industry*, especially the chapter on the State and the introductory chapter prefixed to the edition of 1919.

associations there **must be** a joint body representative of them.

Here a serious objection will almost certainly be encountered. Is not this, it will be asked, merely a very roundabout way of proposing a change in the method of electing the representatives who form the State ? It has often been proposed that the principle of vocational electorates should be partially recognised and incorporated in the constitution side by side with the geographical principle—that, for example, the House of Lords should be replaced by a vocational Second Chamber. It will be suggested that, after all our blare of trumpets, this is what our ' great change ' comes to in the end.

This is not so. There are two absolutely vital differences between the theory which I have been putting forward and the proposal to establish a vocational Second Chamber.

In the first place, the assumption of the ' Vocational Chamber ' theory is that all forms of legislation, no matter what their content, continue to be dealt with by both Chambers and initiated in either. Functional organisation, on the other hand, is explicitly designed to enable each functional body to deal with those matters which belong to its function, without interference in its normal operations from any outside body. Thus, purely political questions belong exclusively to the sphere of the State, purely vocational questions to the sphere of vocational association. It is only when a question affects more than one form of association, that is, affects men in more than one capacity or function, that it is necessary to appeal beyond the purely functional body to some body on which the various functions are represented. The whole basis of functional organisation is designed to enable each functional body to get on with its own job—the job which the members know how to do, and by virtue of their common interest in which they have become associated.

Secondly, the co-ordinating or 'joint' body which I have in mind is less an administrative or legislative body, though it cannot help partaking in some degree of both these characters, than a court of appeal. It does not in the normal case initiate ; it decides. It is not so much a legislature as a constitutional judiciary, or democratic Supreme Court of Functional Equity.

If this is clear, we can return to the question from which we were led into this discussion. Coercion and co-ordination, we said, go hand in hand. If the supreme power of co-ordination rests in the hands of this 'joint' body compounded from the essential functional associations, it seems clear that the supreme power of coercion must rest in the same hands. This involves that the judiciary and the whole paraphernalia of law and police must be under the control of the co-ordinating body.

We saw in the last chapter that the functional organisation of Society necessarily involves the division of power of legislation, as well as of administration, along functional lines. It does not, however, involve a similar division of the judiciary. This question, it will be remembered, we reserved for further treatment, our reason being that it could not be dealt with until we came to discuss the questions of co-ordination and coercion.

The sole possession of a high degree of coercive power, and especially of coercive power of the third kind, which directly affects a man's body, by any single form of functional association, would clearly upset the social balance at which we are aiming, and place the ultimate social power in the hands of that form of association. On the other hand, its possession in an equal degree by each of the essential forms of association would be not only, to say the least of it, inconvenient, and an invitation to the sort of cat-and-dog fight which went on between Church and State in the Middle Ages, but also a denial of the relation of men to associations which is postulated as fundamental in this study. We have seen that a man is a member of an association, not with his whole personality, but with that part of it which he puts into the association in pursuance of the common object which is its function. This being so, the association has at the most no right to coerce the individual in his whole personality, but only in that part of it which he has put into the association. The right to the higher forms of coercion cannot, then, reside either in any one association or in all such associations. It must, however, be in the hands of a single body, if only for reasons of convenience ; and this body can therefore only be the co-ordinating body which is a synthesis of the various essential forms of association.

Even so, there is a strict limit to the coercive power to which even the co-ordinating body is entitled. For, as we have seen, the individual puts into Society, that is into social organisation, not his whole personality, but only those parts of it which can find expression through social organisation. The coercive right of Society as a whole is therefore limited, and there remains a sphere untouched by social organisation in which the individual retains his freedom from coercion.[1] It follows that Society has no right to put any man to death; for death involves a total cessation of personality—on this earth, at any rate.

Even with this safeguard, I rather suspect that many readers have been regarding what has been said in this chapter with a good deal of suspicion and dislike. So much talk about coercion, they will say, augurs ill for the sort of Society which requires it. What is wanted, they will urge, is to get away from the whole idea of coercion as the basis of Society; for it is its coercive character that makes the State such a nasty body.

But it is of no use to refuse to talk about a thing because one does not happen to like it. However much one may dislike coercion and seek to reduce its operation in Society to a minimum, it is necessary to provide for its exercise, if only to supply a means for its abolition. For only that body which possesses coercive power is in a position to forego or prohibit its exercise.

Having discovered where coercive power must reside in a functional Society, we are now in a position to give vent to our dislike of it. One of the greatest results which, I believe, would flow from the full recognition of functional organisation would be a substantial and immediate reduction in the use of coercion in Society. For coercion is the consequence

[1] For a development of this point, see Chapter XII.

of social disorder, and the need for it largely comes, not of innate human wickedness, but of men's failure under existing social conditions to find their proper spheres of social service and to recognise clearly their rights and obligations in Society. If we set our social house in order and make it easier for men to recognise their proper sphere of social service, the need for coercion will, I believe, speedily and progressively disappear.[1]

Moreover, there is another huge advantage of functional Society over State Sovereignty. The theory of the Sovereign State means that the pigmy, man, is confronted by the leviathan, State, which encircles and absorbs him wholly, or at least claims the absolute right to encircle and absorb him. It claims to ' represent ' fully all the individuals who are its members, and therefore to be absolutely superior to them and over them, and to come always first. The functional principle destroys any such claim ; for its denial that the individual can be ' represented ' in any complete sense means that social organisation, however vast and complicated it may be, leaves the individual intact and self-subsistent, distributing his loyalties and obligations among a number of functional bodies, but not absorbed in any or all of them, because outside the sphere of functional organisation there remains always that most vital sphere of individuality whose self-expression is essentially personal and incapable of being organised. The functional principle is,

---

[1] This view appears to be also largely that of Mr. Bertrand Russell, who adopts Guild Socialism as a step towards a non-coercive Society. See his *Roads to Freedom*.

COERCION AND CO-ORDINATION

above all else, the recognition of the absolute and inalienable personal identity of every individual person.[1]

There is one further point with which we must deal before bringing this chapter to an end. In dealing with the nature of the State, we discussed briefly the international aspects of social organisation. We saw that international action, or the external actions of a particular Society, have their various functional aspects, in which they fall within the sphere of the various forms of functional association. There remain those parts of international or external action which involve more than one function or call for action by Society as a whole. Foremost among these there will no doubt leap to the mind of the reader the control of armed forces —the Army, Navy and Air Force. Where, in a functional Society, would the control of these reside ? Who would declare war or make peace or treaties and covenants affecting Society as a whole ? Who would represent a functional Society in a League of Nations ?

The answers to all these questions follow logically from what has already been established. The external use of force and coercion raises similar problems to its internal use, and it is even more manifest in external relations that the right to use it must be concentrated in the hands of a single body. One part of Society cannot be at peace while another

---

[1] For a fuller discussion of this point, see my paper on ' Conflicting Social Obligations ' (*Proceedings of the Aristotelian Society*, 1915-16), and the chapter on ' The Organisation of Freedom ' in my *Labour in the Commonwealth*.

part is at war ; for the claims of war upon the individual citizen are not limited to an eight hours' day, or to the act of voting ; they involve for him the risk of death by violence or starvation. No less clearly is it impossible to entrust external force to any single functional association, both because external affairs involve and interest all the essential forms of association, and because force intended for use externally is also available for internal use, and sole control of armed forces would make the association which possessed it the master of Society. We must, therefore, once more conclude that the external, like the internal, means of coercion, must be in the hands of the body which represents the various social functions, and is entrusted with the task of co-ordination.

Here, again, I am dealing with the problem of external force, not because Armies and Navies and wars are nice things, but because, whether they are nice or nasty, the problem which they present has to be faced. I hope with all my heart that they will disappear before the growth of international co-operation, not only between States, but between all the various forms of functional association. Moreover, I believe that functional association, which has already shown itself far ahead of States in its sense of international solidarity, offers the best hope of a condition of World Society which will make external force unnecessary, and will also persuade everybody, except the incorrigible and disappointed militarists, that it is unnecessary.

Here, then, is the answer to our last question— Who would represent a functional Society on a

COERCION AND CO-ORDINATION

League of Nations ? The answer is that an international Society, which in embryo a League of Nations is, if it is anything more than a sham, would reproduce in itself the functional structure of the smaller Societies composing it. International functional association would undertake, in the wider sphere, the work undertaken in the narrower sphere by national functional organisation, and the central co-ordinating body would reproduce internationally the federal structure of the national co-ordinating bodies. This, no doubt, assumes a certain homogeneity of structure among the Societies composing the League ; but it is at least doubtful whether, without a considerable element of homogeneity, a League of Nations could possibly work. A perception of this perhaps accounts for the desire of the ' Sovereign States,' which have just formed a League, to impress upon all candidates for entry the particular structure, economic and political, which they themselves possess.[1]

[1] This point is further discussed in my *Labour in the Commonwealth*, chap. ii.

CHAPTER IX

THE ECONOMIC STRUCTURE OF SOCIETY

THERE will be a certain type of reader who will regard the greater part of this book as beside the point, or at best as a harmless form of theoretical diversion. I am ignoring, he will say, or relegating to a quite secondary position the factor which in reality dominates and determines the whole course of social organisation. Political organisation, and indeed every essential form of associative life, is, in his view, the result of economic conditions and of the distribution of economic power in the community, and the changes which occur from time to time in social organisation are equally the results of changes in the economic circumstances. In the words of Marx and Engels, "The economic structure of Society is the real basis on which the juridical and political superstructure is raised—in short, the mode of production determines the character of the social, political, and intellectual life generally."

It is necessary for us to take notice of this point of view, and to admit at once the large measure of truth which it possesses, if our exposition of the theoretical basis of Society is to have any vital contact with the working of actual Societies. Indeed, we have already, at several stages of our argument, laid stress on the vital importance of the economic factor in influencing and directing the working of other forms of association, as well as the interaction of various economic factors and associations. We have, however, always treated the influence of economic factors upon non-economic forms of association as a form of *perversion*, leading to a failure of the association so affected to fulfil its proper function in Society. If the Marxian thesis is right in its entirety, we must abandon this view ; for it is folly to regard as ' perversion ' a phenomenon which flows directly from the nature of Society itself, or to treat as independent forms of association bodies and manifestations which are only the ' superstructure ' of economic organisation.

In fact, we are here faced by a theory which is the complete inversion of the theory of State Sovereignty which we have already rejected. Having pulled down the State from its pedestal, we are asked to install the economic structure of Society in its place. There is, however, a profound difference in the argument advanced. Although the claim of the State to Sovereignty is sometimes based on the fact that it is the sole repository of armed force, this argument is not very often or very persistently employed ; for it is clear that there is no reason in the nature of the State why it should occupy this position, and also increasingly clear that there exist other forms of ' force,' such as the strike, which may under favourable conditions successfully challenge even a monopolist in armed force. The case for State Sovereignty is therefore usually argued not on this basis of *fact*, but on what is put forward as a basis of *right*. The State is said to be sovereign, because it represents everybody.

The argument that the economic structure of Society is, if I may use the term, ' sovereign,' is based on quite different grounds. It is not as a rule suggested that economic conditions *ought* to be the supreme determinant in Society, but only that they are and must be, owing to the operation of forces beyond our control. The advocates of this theory—the ' materialist ' or ' economic ' conception of history—are indeed apt to be impatient of ' oughts ' and rights. They claim that their conception is ' scientific,' and base it upon the stern laws of necessity and material evolution. Whatever fine theories other people may spin, they continue to proclaim the hard fact that the human race marches upon its belly, and that the economic order of Society determines everything else.

Whatever the process of argument, the result arrived at is in one respect the same as that arrived at by the advocates of State Sovereignty. Functional organisation in either case disappears, or appears only as a subordinate form determined by and existing on the sufferance of a single form of organisation, which, even if it has a functional basis, is not in its operation confined to any particular function.

There is, however, still an ambiguity in the materialist conception. What is meant by the

words, " the economic structure of Society " ?   Do
they refer to actual associations, such as Trade
Unions or capitalist associations, and to the distribution of power among such associations ?   Or do
they, as the final clause of our quotation from Marx
and Engels rather seems to suggest, refer to the
actual material conditions existing in Society,
without regard to the associations which are
related to these conditions ?

There is no doubt that the direct reference is not
to associations but to the material conditions
themselves.   But it is held that each set of material
conditions finds its necessary expression in a set of
associations and a form of social organisation of its
own.   Thus, one set of associations corresponded to,
and arose out of, the productive conditions of
primitive Society ; another set was the inevitable
result of the productive conditions of the Middle
Ages ; and yet another set, under which we are
now living, has been called into existence by the
great inventions and the development of large-
scale production which marked the period of the
Industrial Revolution.   Each set of economic conditions changes gradually, with or without a sharp
break or upheaval at some point, into the next,
and each new set of associations grows and is built
up gradually within the old, until the conditions
are ripe for it to assert its dominance, and for the
obsolete set of associations to be discarded.   Thus,
within the capitalist system, a new set of associations is being built up which will take the place of
Capitalism ; but those new associations, Trade
Unions and other working-class bodies, are as much

the products of economic conditions as the capitalist system itself.

As an analysis of the growth of Capitalism, and of the working of capitalist institutions both in the past and at the present time, this theory is so largely right that the points at which it is wrong are easily overlooked. Yet there are at least two considerable mis-statements involved in it, as it is most commonly expressed.

In the first place, it does not prove, as is often contended, that the *form* of non-economic associations is determined by economic conditions, but only that their actual *working* and methods of operation are so determined. Thus, when a prominent Marxist[1] writes a book to prove that the State as an association is the political expression of Capitalism and will disappear with the overthrow of Capitalism, what he actually does prove is that, while Capitalism exists as the dominant social form, the State will be forced to do the bidding of Capitalism, and will be, in actual fact, the political expression of the dominant economic power of the capitalist classes. What he does not prove is that, with the overthrow of Capitalism, the State will disappear ; or that it will not be able to assume and exercise its true function as soon as the economic pressure of Capitalism is removed.

In other words, his argument does not in any sense disprove our thesis that what occurs under Capitalism is a *perversion* of the true function of the State, and its use, not as a political instrument of the whole people, but as a secondary economico-

[1] *The State : its Origin and Function.* By William Paul.

political instrument by the dominant economic class.

Secondly, although the State is in fact largely an ' Executive Committee for administering the affairs of the capitalist class,' it is not exclusively so. Perversion of function is not carried so far as to obliterate all signs and traces of its real function. Indeed, by examining the actual working of the State, even under capitalist conditions, we have been able to assign to it its essential function in a rationally ordered Society Under any economic system the State will continue to exercise functions which are not economic, and the perversion of its activities by economic causes will not extend continuously to all its doings.

It will be seen that the line of argument which I am adopting is an endorsement of a large part of the Marxian case. While I cannot accept the neo-Marxian criticism of the State as universally true, or as touching the State in its real social function, I am accepting its general truth as it applies to the State of to-day. It is the case that the functioning, not only of the State, but also of most other forms of association, including the economic forms themselves perhaps more than any, is perverted by the influence exercised upon them by economic factors.

Nor is the reason for this widespread perversion far to seek. It is embedded in the present economic structure of Society. For, instead of being organised as a coherent whole for the complementary performance of social functions, men are to-day organised in the economic sphere in conflicting groups, each of which is at least as much concerned with getting the better of the others and diverting to its own use as much as possible of the product of labour as with serving the community by the performance of a useful function. Thus the economic sphere of social action has become a battle-ground of contending sections, and these combatants are also irresistibly impelled to widen their battle-front so as to lay waste the tracts of social organisation which lie outside the economic sphere. Thus, trade rivalries lead to wars between nations; internal industrial dissension leads employers' associations and Trade Unions to seek direct representation in Parliament, and to extend into the political sphere their economic disputes; and finally, the whole people tends to rally to the one standard or the other, and to make Society as a whole a 'devastated area' of economic conflict and class-war.

I am not concerned to insist here on my belief that Labour is in the right, and Capitalism in the wrong in this struggle, but solely to insist that, wherever the right lies, the existence of such an economic conflict in Society is fatal to the due performance of its function by each form of social organisation. Indeed, this statement can be made more general; for economic conflict is not the only sort of division that can so rend a community asunder as largely to stop the functioning of its various parts. Religious differences, as we shall see later, can produce and have produced the same results, and there is no final reason why some other matter of discord should not produce them if it arouses strong enough feelings in a sufficient part of the population. We may say, then, that the existence of a profound social cleavage in regard to the fulfilment of any essential social function is prejudicial, and may be fatal, to the performance of its proper function by each form of social organisation.

In our own Society at least, and in the larger industrialised communities generally, economic divisions are at the present time the principal obstacles to the fulfilment of social functions. Great inequalities of wealth and economic status lead inevitably, under the modern conditions which necessarily favour large-scale combination on both sides, to cleavages in Society that are bound to assume the character of open conflicts. It is therefore useless to expect that the various forms of association will perform their functions properly as long as the conditions which make for such conflicts continue in existence. The only remedy lies in some form of approximate, or comparatively economic equality.

It must be made clear that this assertion is not a plea for, or a declaration of faith in, any particular economic system, even if faith in a particular system is implied in much of this book. Comparative or approximate economic equality is possible under more than one system, and I am Marxian enough to believe that different systems are required for its attainment under different economic and productive systems. Thus, a generally diffused system of peasant proprietorship, such as Mr. Belloc and his followers have made an undeniably heroic theoretical attempt to adapt to the conditions of modern industrialised Societies,[1] is certainly a possible approximation to equality for an agrarian Society, and under it such a Society might hope to find its various functional associations doing their jobs with some approximation to propriety. All the various schools of Socialist thought—Collectivist, Communist, Guild Socialist, Syndicalist—set out to provide a basis for economic equality on the opposite principle, not of the general diffusion and distribution, but of the concentration and social ownership of the means of production. Any of these systems, whatever their other faults, might, given an appropriate set of material conditions as a basis, provide economic equality and thereby make possible the functioning of Society without perversion from economic causes. But without virtual economic equality it is useless to look for the disappearance or subordination of class-conflict, and therefore useless to expect Society to function aright, either economically or in any other sphere.

In granting so much to the ' materialists,' however, we must be careful to make clear what we do not grant. Although Society does in one sense walk upon its belly, it does not by any means follow either that the things of the belly must always be Society's main concern, or that they will always continue to dominate and determine the other forms of social action. Far from it. The present dominance of economic considerations in Society is based on two things—the ' struggle for bread ' and the ' struggle for power.' In the struggle for

[1] See *The Servile State*, by Hilaire Belloc, and *The Real Democracy*, by J. E. F. Mann, N. J. Sievers, and R. W. T. Cox.

bread there are two factors—shortage and mal-distribution—to be considered. In so far as productive power falls short, and there is a real deficiency in the supply of commodities to supply real needs, there exists an economic problem which will continue to trouble us whatever social system we may adopt, until we find a remedy in increasing production. But in so far as productive power is adequate, but difficulty arises over the division of the product, *i.e.* mal-distribution, the problem disappears with the realisation of economic equality. And with the disappearance of this problem goes also one of the two causes which make the economic factors dominate the other factors in social organisation.

The second cause, the 'struggle for power,' remains. This is not exclusively or in its nature economic; but it manifests itself in the economic sphere in a struggle between economic classes for the control of industry. With the abolition of economic class, and the establishment of unified functional control of industries by all the persons engaged in them, the social struggle for economic power also disappears, and the second cause of the predominance of economic factors is also removed. In other words, democratic functional organisation and approximate economic equality are the conditions of the removal of the dominance of economic factors in Society.

In short, if economic classes and class-conflicts are done away with, the Marxian thesis will no longer hold good, and economic power will no longer be the dominant factor in Society. Economic considerations will lose their unreal and distorted magnitude in men's eyes, and will retain their place as one group among others round which the necessary social functions are centred. For the artificial material valuation of social things, which is forced upon us by the actual structure of present-day Society, it will become possible to substitute a spiritual valuation. When once we have got the economic sphere of social action reasonably organised on functional lines, we shall be free to forget about it most of the time, and to interest ourselves in other matters. The economic sphere will not, of course, be any less essential than before ; but it will need less attention. Always associations and institutions, as well as people, need most attention when they are least ' themselves.' Our preoccupation with economics occurs only because the economic system is diseased.

Needless to say, the organisation of the ' economic substratum ' of Society on functional lines would produce a very different economic organisation from that which exists in Society at the present time. To-day, almost all the economic forms of association are doubled with counter-association of workers responding to association of employers, often with associations of managers and professionals trying to steer an awkward course between these persistent Symplegades. All this duplication of associations is not merely wasteful, but actively pernicious. It means that energy, which is required for the service of the community, is diverted and perverted into a conflict which, from the standpoint of the community, produces nothing.

ECONOMIC STRUCTURE OF SOCIETY

This is not to condemn those who engage in, or actively stir up, such conflict. The class-divisions and economic inequalities which exist in Society make the conflict not merely inevitable, but the only means to the attainment of better conditions. It has been truly said that there is no instance in history of a dominant economic class giving up its position except under the pressure of a rising economic class which has become stronger than itself. The only end to this process is the abolition of economic classes and the realisation of economic equality.

The economic structure of Society can only be properly adjusted to the due performance of its function when the elements of conflict, and with them the conflicting forms of economic association, are resolved into a functional unity. This would involve the disappearance of some, and the radical reorganisation and re-orientation of others, of the existing types of economic association. The employers' association and the Trade Union would alike be out of place as primarily offensive and defensive forms of organisation, and the main types of association would find their motive not in defence or offence, but in social service. The personnel of industry would no longer be divided into opposing camps, but united in its common pursuit of its function of the social organisation of production.

If this chapter seems altogether too general and unsubstantial to be a real analysis or criticism of the economic part of the social structure, that is because I am loth, by plunging into details of present-day organisation, to overweight this book with controversies which are irrelevant to its central purpose. I am trying to speak in general terms, leaving the application to be made, and the moral to be pointed, by others or in other bodies. I have therefore not attempted to describe the present or past or future economic organisation of Society, but only to point out where economic conditions and organisation do, and do not, affect the structure and working of Society as a whole. Ordinary ' political theory ' has suffered immeasurably from its ignoring of the economic aspects and structure of the social system, while Marxian theory suffers from its persistent identification of the economic structure with Society as a whole. I have tried to avoid both these mistakes, and at the same time to recognise the vast influence which economic conditions must always have upon the character of social organisation as a whole, and to point out wherein it seems to me this influence would be limited and made definite under a system of economic equality.

There are economic arguments and moral arguments enough in favour of the adoption of the principle of equality in the economic sphere. With these arguments I am not here concerned. I have tried only to start the argument for economic equality from the standpoint of social theory and social organisation. In conclusion, let me restate this argument in a single sentence.

The existence of economic inequality means that each form of association in Society, instead of attending to the fulfilment of its own social function, is perverted to serve economic ends, and that thereby the whole balance and coherence of Society are destroyed, and, in the last resort, revolution is converted from a menace, into a necessity for the restoration of a reasonable social system.

CHAPTER X

REGIONALISM AND LOCAL GOVERNMENT

IN our treatment of the State in earlier chapters, we explicitly reserved for later consideration the question of local government. One good reason for adopting this course was that the question of local organisation arises not only in relation to the political structure of Society, but also in relation to its economic structure and to the structure of every functional form of association. For us, the problem of local government is not merely a problem of the relations between the State and the ' local authorities,' but of the whole organisation of Society over larger and smaller geographical areas.

It is being realised to an increasing extent that the problem of the areas of government and administration is not a purely political question, but also raises at once many economic issues. Thus, it is often made a cause of complaint against the existing areas of local government that they do not correspond to economic requirements. An efficient tramway service needs to serve the areas of several neighbouring towns as well as the rural districts between them ; the supply of water and other public utility services could be better administered if the areas of local government were enlarged ; what has grown to be essentially a single city is often divided into several boroughs with their separate administrations ; a town or city is constantly faced with the overflow of its suburbs into the areas of surrounding authorities. Similarly, in the purely economic sphere, we have schemes for the regionalisation of the coal-mining industry under big regional trusts.[1]

These are only a few instances of the insistence with which the problem of areas is forcing itself upon our consideration at the present time. Here, we are not concerned directly with the solution of these particular difficulties, but with the general problem of the areas of functional administration, and the relations of larger and smaller areas within a given Society. Clearly, the tendency at the present time is for the areas of administration to enlarge themselves continually in response to the growth in the scale of production and to the continual expansion, and ' running into one another,' of the growing towns and urban areas.

The case for the preservation of small areas and units of government has been again and again clearly and forcibly stated. It has been pointed out that, as areas grow larger, the direct contact between the representative and the represented tends to disappear, and the unreality of representation grows

[1] For the economic difficulties involved in existing areas of local government, see *State and Municipal Enterprise*, by S. and B. Webb (Labour Research Department) ; and for regionalisation of coal mines, see Sir A. Duckham's scheme in the Reports of the Coal Industry Commission.

greater and more evident. Rousseau held that democracy was only possible in small Societies, because only in small Societies could the people as a whole retain its control over the conduct of affairs. Mr. Penty and the craftsmen, Mr. Chesterton in *The Napoleon of Notting Hill*, and other and graver authorities, have put the case for the small unit as the human unit which makes possible a spirit of neighbourhood and unity which is difficult to attain over larger areas. The followers of Professor Patrick Geddes have infused into their conception of ' Town-Planning ' the love of the small area. It is, I think, true that, in the long run at least, to allow ' local patriotism ' and local organisation to fall into decay and disrepute is to imperil the whole basis on which Society rests.

It is a commonplace at the present time that local feeling is in decay. Indeed, the constant attempts to discover ' revivals ' of it and to stimulate it into action serve to show how serious the decay is. Even where local feeling remains strong and vigorous, as in many parts of Great Britain it does, it has, nevertheless, withdrawn itself largely from the sphere of local government, or local economic administration, and concentrated itself round the less organised and unorganised parts of local life— sport, for instance, and sociability in general. This is a perilous situation for the community ; for, under right conditions, local feeling ought to express itself not only in these largely personal spheres, but also in all the spheres of organised social administration.

Regionalism, as I understand it, is primarily an

REGIONALISM

attempt to face this difficulty, and by making local areas real areas, to restore the influence of local spirit upon the work of social administration. It is an attempt to define areas which are at once units of social feeling and, as far as possible, also areas of economic life, and suitable to serve as units for the work of administration. The chief faults of most of the existing areas are two : their unreality as centres of local feeling, and their inadequacy to the work of administration under modern conditions, in relation not only to local transport and other public utility services, but also to public health, education, and most of the other work of local government.

If these two faults admit of a single remedy, so much the better ; and clearly the views of the regionalists and of those who think with them in this matter have every claim to be fully considered by a Society which is admittedly sick and ill at ease with its existing areas.

But what must strike us at once is the fact that the regionalist proposal may appear in two contrary lights. From one point of view, it appears as a proposal for the drastic enlargement of the present areas of local administration, while from another point of view it appears as a scheme of devolution, or more, designed to reduce the area of administration in respect of many of those matters which are now dealt with centrally by the State.

Thus, we see that we cannot treat the problem of areas in isolation from the content of their administration—from their powers and the questions with which they are concerned. Under the existing, and indeed under any system, some things will be administered centrally and some locally. This would be the case also if ' regions ' were adopted as important units of administration. The problem is thus complex, and involves a combined consideration of areas and powers.

Before we consider this problem directly, it is necessary to point out that the whole question assumes rather a different form in a functionally organised Society from that which it has under the existing conditions of local and central government. For the objection that the representative loses touch with, and cannot be controlled by, those whom he represents in a large area, though it still has force, is far less applicable when the function of the representative is clearly defined than where it is vague or general. A functionally organised Society can therefore maintain its democratic character over a larger area than a Society organised on the pattern of State Sovereignty, or, for that matter, than a Society organised on the basis of Marxian industrialism. If it is inconvenient to restrict the size of an area, it may be possible to preserve democracy by restricting the function, and at the same time increasing the number of representative bodies in the larger area.

Thus, while it might be dangerous to enlarge the areas of local government in industry and politics under existing conditions, I believe that the ' region ' would be, for many of the most important purposes, the best area of local government in a functionally organised Society. The unit of local government, to be effective, must be at once small enough to be democratically controlled, and a real unit of social life and feeling. An area which would be too large under a non-functional system might be just the right size for democratic and efficient functional administration.

But what of Regionalism as a proposal to substitute, for many purposes, the smaller area of the ' region ' for the larger area of the State or the national economic organisation ? I believe that this proposal is largely right because, in most cases, the area [1] of present-day States is simply too large for effective or democratic organisation of most things under any system, however functional. This does not mean that the present State areas have no reality and no use ; but only that many matters which are now administered naturally would be better administered over a smaller area. The larger areas—those which are larger than the ' region ' or ' province '—seem to be marked out as spheres rather of co-ordinating activity on most questions than of actual executive direction.

If, as I believe, both economic life and social life generally call for ' regional ' organisation and for the centring in the region of the largest measure of actual executive authority, two groups of questions at once arise. First, what is the proper relation of the economic or political ' region ' to the larger groups of which it forms a part, and to the smaller groups which form part of it ? And secondly, is

---

[1] Here and elsewhere I use the word ' area,' not to denote so many square miles, but a complex involving various considerations, including the extent, population, economic and general character of the country, psychology of the inhabitants, etc.

there any principle which can serve as at least a general indication of the respective spheres of the various ' sizes ' of administrative or governmental unit ?

The first group of questions at once raises the problem of federalism, decentralisation, or some other form of allocation of powers. Broadly speaking, there are in operation in different places three different systems, in addition to all manner of variations upon them, of determining the relations between larger and smaller authorities of the same type within a single Society. First, there is *federalism* in the strict sense, under which all authority is finally vested in the smaller bodies severally, and each of these hands over certain definite powers to the larger body, retaining in its own hands all powers not specifically transferred. Secondly, there is *decentralisation* or *centralisation*, in which all power is credited originally to the larger body, which doles out with greater or less generosity such powers as it thinks fit to the smaller bodies. English local government, in so far as it rests upon statute law, belongs to this type. Thirdly, there is the form in which the power is originally divided between the larger and the smaller bodies, special powers being reserved to each. This occurs principally in the case of written constitutions, and especially under systems of Dominion Home Rule in the British Empire. Such intermediate systems are generally worded either in federal terms (as in the case of Australia) or in unitary terms (as in the case of Canada) ; but the wording makes little difference to the result. Such mixed systems really constitute a third type.

REGIONALISM

In the sphere of political government, in which alone there is evidence enough to go upon, both constitutions originally federal and constitutions originally unitary tend to approximate as the result of experience of present-day conditions to this third, or mixed, type. The reason is obvious. The relation between larger and smaller bodies of the same kind is increasingly defining itself in terms not of powers alone, but of powers in relation to functions. It is for the larger body to fulfil certain functions, and for the smaller bodies to fulfil certain others. The question of local and central government is not, in fact, primarily a question between federalism and decentralisation, but a question of a right allocation of social functions.

This is true as regards the ends to be attained and the actual balance to be sought ; but it is not true to the same extent of the methods to be used. The methods are, in fact, prescribed by the circumstances. If there exists a large ' unitarily ' administered area which requires to be broken up for the performance of some of its functions, the method of decentralisation will normally be the most convenient method both of breaking it up, and of setting up new ' regional ' bodies where they are required. If, on the other hand, it is desired to bind together a number of unco-ordinated small bodies into a larger unit, federation is often the easiest instrument to use, at least in the earlier stages. The method is a matter of temporary expediency, and differing methods are needed in different circumstances for arriving at the same end.

Not so with the end itself. Before we can begin

to think about methods, we must know, as something comparatively fixed and definite, the end to which we desire to attain. We must make up our minds what, for our Society and generation, is the most desirable division of functions between larger and smaller bodies within it, and we must then discover the methods best suited to promote the realisation of this object.

I believe that, in a functionally organised Society, the great bulk of the administrative work, both politically and economically, will best be done 'regionally,' that is by political and economic bodies intermediate in extent between the national State and the existing local authorities.[1] Were some such principle adopted, and twenty or thirty such areas brought into administrative existence in England, I believe that the functions which would still be best executed by the big natural unit would be chiefly functions of co-ordination, apart from a few big groups of questions, both economic and political, in which national uniformity of treatment would continue to be essential.

It must be borne in mind that I am speaking here not of a single national body, the State, and of a single local or rather 'regional' body in each 'region,' but of a number of national functional

[1] The 'region,' in the sense in which I use the word, is not so large as the 'province' contemplated in most schemes of English 'Provincial Home Rule,' or in plans for a 'New Heptarchy'; but it is considerably larger than most of the existing areas of local government. I believe England could reasonably be divided into, say, twenty or thirty regions, most of which would be real social units and local feeling, and many of which would be also approximately economic units.

bodies in the national area, and of a number of regional functional bodies in the 'region.' The problem has its different aspects—that of co-ordinating the working of regional economic bodies on the one hand, and that of co-ordinating regional political bodies on the other. The problem of co-ordinating political with economic bodies we have already discussed, and our treatment of that subject in Chapter VIII. holds good of the 'region' as well as of the national area.

If co-ordination is to be the main function of the national bodies, what is the best method of representation upon them? There seem to be, broadly speaking, two possibilities—one, the method now adopted for electing Parliaments and many other national bodies, by universal suffrage in geographical constituencies with or without Proportional Representation, or various other devices for making representation more true or the reverse—the other, the method of indirect electing, under which the members of the national bodies are chosen by the bodies of the same kind covering a smaller area, the members of a national assembly by the various regional assemblies of the same kind for example. Where the main duty of a national body is that of co-ordination within a clearly defined sphere, I am inclined to believe that the second method will be found to be the best. Under a regional system, the direct control of the elector would be over his representatives on the various functional bodies within the 'region,' and it would be best for these in turn to control, and where necessary recall, their representatives on the various national co-ordinating bodies.

I do not, however, desire to suggest that this indirect form of election would necessarily apply to every national body. The method of election that is best varies with the function of the body concerned, and, if a national body exercises large powers of direct administration or government, or deals with matters for which there is no corresponding regional body, direct election is obviously available as an alternative.

It will be seen that, in local as in national affairs, the arguments advanced in this book favour the *ad hoc* principle. Indeed, they favour it in two ways, by insisting on the need for a clear definition of the function of each representative body, which is the distinguishing mark of an *ad hoc* authority, and also by insisting on an *ad hoc* electorate, so that everybody votes for a body in which all are directly concerned, but vocational and other special or selective electorates are adopted in other cases. Provided the functions of the body are clearly defined, and the right electorate secured, all the advantages lie with the *ad hoc* body over the *omnibus* authority, which is based upon the fallacious theory of representation which we have already discarded.

I have laid stress on the importance of the ' region ' as an administrative and governmental area for political and economic purposes alike. I do not mean by this to imply that it is always necessary, or possible, to adopt exactly the same area as the unit for all the various social functions. Thus, in a particular part of a country, the limit of social feeling may be so clearly marked as to leave no possible doubt as to the proper boundaries for

REGIONALISM

a particular political 'region.' But, while this is so, it may be quite clear that this political 'region' will not do for an economic 'region,' and the economic boundaries may be no less distinctly, but at the same time differently, defined. In such a case, it will be necessary to adopt different areas for the political and the economic region. It is, however, desirable that the areas of administration for the various functions should coincide wherever possible, in order to make easy co-operation between the various functional bodies within a district. The areas ought to coincide wherever possible, and, where they differ, ought to overlap as little as possible. Thus, where they cannot be made to coincide, it may be possible to make the area of two 'regions' dealing with one function coincide with the area of one 'region' dealing with another.

I cannot close this chapter without asserting, with all the vehemence at my command, the vital importance to the larger community of the maintenance of strong local life and feeling throughout the smaller communities within it. Only if men can learn the social spirit in their daily contact with their neighbours can they hope to be good citizens of the larger community. Co-operation begins at home, and the fact that we often quarrel most fiercely with our nearest friends and neighbours is only a further indication of this truth. For hate, like love, is a thing of the emotions, and it is upon the emotions that the possibility of real human co-operation is based. The local spirit of a community is the key to its national spirit.

The existing local bodies mostly fall between two

stools. They are neither small enough to appeal to the spirit of ' neighbourliness ' nor large enough to form effective units of political or economic administrations, or to appeal to that larger local spirit which characterises the man of the West Country, or the Lancastrian, or the Yorkshireman.[1] The ' region ' will be large enough to be efficient and to make this larger appeal. But the smaller appeal will still need to be made, and I believe that the adoption of regional areas would open the way for a revival of very much smaller local areas which, without possessing important administrative functions, would act as centres round which the feelings of ' neighbourliness ' could find expression, and also as most valuable organs of criticism through which a fire of praise, blame and advice could be brought to bear upon the representatives on the regional bodies. Such smaller centres of feeling and expression are no less vital to real democracy than the larger bodies upon which, under present conditions, most of the work of administration is bound to fall.

It should be noted that, throughout this chapter, the treatment of the question of ' Regionalism ' is theoretical and is not conceived in terms of practical proposals for immediate adoption. I am speaking, not of changes which can readily be introduced into Society as it is at present constituted, but of the form which local government might reasonably be expected to assume in a functionally organised Society. At present, Society

[1] The County Council is not a unit, but a residuum with the heart cut out of it by the severance of the towns.

REGIONALISM

is largely a battle-ground of opposing social forces, especially in the economic sphere. This fact inevitably forces upon associations, and above all upon economic associations, a growing concentration upon both sides ; for each tries to roll up bigger battalions with which to confront the big battalions of its adversary. Thus, both capitalist associations and Trade Unions tend to an increasing extent to centralise their activities upon at least a national scale, not because the national area is the best area for most forms of economic administration, but because they are less concerned with efficient service than with sectional or ' class ' aims, and with their mutual struggle. These conditions, making for centralisation, are likely to persist as long as the existing diversion of the community into opposing economic classes continues. It is therefore probable that most regionalist proposals, especially in their economic aspects, will only become ' practical politics ' when the existing class-divisions in industry have disappeared.

CHAPTER XI

CHURCHES

IT is impossible, in any study of social theory which professes to be in any sense comprehensive, not to deal directly with the place of religious associations in Society. The old quarrel of Church and State may belong mainly to the past, and may have ceased, in this country at least, to affect profoundly the whole social order; but the place of Churches in modern Society is by no means settled, and, apart from this controversy, Churches occupy a position of essential importance in the Society of to-day. Not only is the Roman International still with us: the Church of England and the 'Free Churches' of this country have been in our own day centres of important social controversy, and, as we saw in our first chapter,[1] sources from which new conceptions of the functional organisation of Society have flowed.

In the past, and especially in the Middle Ages, the controversy between Church and State centred mainly round the question of temporal power—a controversy dependent upon the papal claim to a vice-regency of God over all the Societies of Christendom. To-day, the controversy is not in the

[1] See p. 10.

main about temporal power, but about the relations which should exist between Church and State in the sphere of spiritual power. Thus, the Establishment, regarded by its adherents as a recognition by the State of the spiritual mission and social function of the Church, is in fact also an instrument of State supremacy over the Church, a means whereby the temporal power of the State, often wielded now by persons who are not Churchmen, takes into its hand the appointment of spiritual leaders. In return for a doubtful gain in status, the Established Church surrenders a precious part of its autonomy— a position which only continues because the Establishment now does no particular harm to persons who are not Churchmen, while Churchmen cling to it either from a sense that it confers or recognises status, or from less worthy economic motives. Thus, the growing 'Life and Liberty Movement' in the Church of England recognises to the full the need for spiritual autonomy, but still clings to Establishment, which, under the conditions of to-day, cannot be made consistent with autonomy.

In so far as 'establishment' is to be regarded as a social recognition of the mission of the 'established' body, it appears to be quite logical where, and as long as, the vast majority of the people owe allegiance to a single Church. It is logical in such circumstances, because the Church cannot concern itself solely with purely 'private' concerns, but must also, if it is to have a mission at all, concern itself intimately and constantly with men's social and associative existence. Its rules and precepts of conduct, if they apply at all, must apply not only to men's private and personal doings, but also to their social doings and to the doings of the associations of which they are members. No Church which claims to have any influence upon conduct can be merely ' other-worldly ' : indeed, it can only be effectively ' other-worldly ' in proportion as it occupies itself with the things of this world.

This social character of Churches, implicit in their very nature and explicit wherever they have any real hold upon the people, carries with it the right to the recognition of Churches as an integral part of the structure of Society, wherever a considerable proportion of the people is concerned with them. But ' establishment ' has so far meant the exclusive recognition of the social character of a single Church within a single territory, whether or not it is the only Church or the Church which is generally accepted by the people. If, however, the right to recognition depends upon the social character of Churches, that right extends to all Churches which possess this character. The functional principle implies the recognition of all Churches on a basis of equality.

Here, however, an immediate difficulty confronts us. The social recognition of the Miners' Federation or of the Edinburgh School Board does not preclude the social recognition of the National Union of Railwaymen or the School Board of Dundee. Indeed, it even implies it ; for the functions of various industries and of various local authorities are complementary, and form a basis for co-operation and the creation of joint and federal bodies where they are required for the functioning and social recognition of any particular form of association. Churches, on the other hand, despite attempts at ' Reunion All Round ' are not professedly complementary and do not naturally cohere ; for almost every one of them professes, and must be taken as believing itself, to be the only true Church.

The problem of ' recognition,' then, is not so simple in the case of Churches as in the case of those forms of association which cohere naturally, because they recognise at once the complementary character of their social functions.

What, then, is the right of Churches to recognition to mean in practice in a functionally organised Society ? Or, in other words, what is the right relation of Churches in such a Society not merely to the State, but to the various essential forms of association and to the bodies which exist to co-ordinate their work ?

We cannot hope to answer this question until we have studied more carefully the nature of the Church as a form of human association. As soon as we do this, its essential difference from the other forms of association which we have been mainly considering becomes at once manifest. The ' functions ' of which we have been speaking throughout this book we have again and again interpreted as meaning ' getting something done,' that is, producing material results external to the persons who are members of the associations. I do not mean that Churches never aim at material results, any more than I mean that political and economic associa- tions have no spiritual aspects, or aim at results that are merely material. But I do mean that the direct objects of political and economic association are primarily material, whereas the direct objects of Churches are primarily spiritual.

This fact can perhaps be stated more clearly in another way. The distinction between political and economic association is that they have different jobs to do, and work upon different subject-matters. But Churches must concern themselves with the subject-matter of both political and economic associations, as well as with many matters which fall outside their sphere. The distinction between Churches and these other forms of association lies, then, not in the subject-matter with which they deal, but in their different ways of approaching it. They are concerned with producing a material result, and Churches are also concerned in producing this result ; but with political and economic associations the result is primary, while with Churches it is secondary and derivative. The primary concern of Churches, as social associations, is to make their conception of the Spirit of God manifest and real upon earth.

The appeal, then, of Churches is different, and the form of social power proper to them is different. The power of political and economic associations is a material power, exercisable in the last resort upon the bodies of the members : the power of Churches is or ought to be a spiritual power, exercisable upon the mind and not upon the body.

If this is so, it follows that Churches can form no part of the co-ordinating body in Society, in so far as this body is concerned with material forms of coercion. Material coercion, despite the rack and the stake, is no business of Churches. May the time come when it will cease to be the business of Society in any aspect.

Our problem now reappears as a problem of the relation of spiritual to material power. And we arrive at once at the result that these two forms of power possess no organisable relation. If there is to be an organised relation between Churches and the other forms of association of which we have been speaking, it can arise only in two cases, where the Churches are directly concerned with material things and where their other associations are directly concerned with spiritual things.

In fact, the proper relation of Churches to political and economic forms of association is essentially one of co-operation without formal co-ordination. Churches cannot, without sacrificing their essentially spiritual character, enter into, or become a part of, the co-ordinating structure of Society dealt with in Chapter VIII. But they can, on many issues, fruitfully co-operate with other associations. An instance is the civil recognition of religious marriages which exists to-day. Co-operation is essential : co-ordination a distortion of the character both of Churches and of the bodies with which the co-ordination is made.

This separation of Church and State is in no sense either an isolation of the Churches or a derogation from their social character. It is not an isolation, because the need for full co-operation remains : it is not a derogation, because it is the very fact that the Church—any real Church—is a *universitas* in itself that makes co-ordination impossible. Full liberty of religious association and observance is therefore not the sole necessity: full self-government for every Church and complete freedom from interference with its management, appointments, doctrines and spiritual conduct is also implied. Only through such separation can Churches be freed for the attainment of the fullest liberty and the proper performance of their spiritual function. Political and economic associations must make their laws and Churches theirs. They may differ and even be contradictory; but they cannot conflict because they are on different planes, and, where they are contradictory, it is for the individual to choose his allegiance. History proves that he will often prefer a material penalty to a spiritual reprobation.

Nothing that has been said in this chapter is meant to suggest that the organised Churches possess a monopoly of the spiritual function, or that they are the sole depositories of spiritual wisdom. As in other spheres, the individual is the ultimate depository of spiritual wisdom and unwisdom, and only a part of his ' wisdom ' is susceptible of organisation. The existence of Churches is only one of the objective symbols of the truth that every material thing and purpose is also spiritual, and their separate existence does not derogate from, but serves to emphasise, the spiritual as well as material character of other associations. As in man, so in Society and in the community, the spiritual and material ' universes ' exist side by side, related in a relation which, fundamental and necessary as it is, is no easier to explain in the one case than in the other. Much that is spiritual escapes the organising influence of all the Churches, as much that is material escapes the organising of political, economic and other primarily material forms of association; in the spiritual, as in every other sphere, the individual remains as the ultimate reality in which all association is built, but whom association can never exhaust or completely express.

CHAPTER XII

LIBERTY

THIS book has throughout dealt mainly with the functions and interrelations of associations within the community, with the nature of association, and with its various forms and motives, with the problems arising out of the actual working of associations, and so on. In short, it has been mainly a book about organised Society, and has only dealt incidentally and in passing with those aspects of community which fall outside the sphere of organised Society.

This, however, does not absolve us from the necessity of dealing, from our own standpoint, with the problem which has presented the greatest difficulty of all to every social theorist—the problem of the relation of the individual to Society, and of the place of individual liberty in the community.

The problem does not, indeed, assume for us the form which it assumed for Herbert Spencer, the form simply expressed in the phrase ' the Man *versus* the State ' ; but neither can we be content with the simple identification of liberty with law to which some theorists of an opposite school have all too willingly approximated. The question for us is one, first, of the relative spheres of social and individual

LIBERTY

action, and secondly, one of the relation of the individual to the various associations of which he is a member, or which claim in Society a jurisdiction which affects his interests.

This forces upon us some attempt to define liberty, as it appears in Society and in the community. And here the first thing we have to do is to get clear in our minds a distinction between two senses in which the word is used—liberty attaching to the individual *qua* individual, and liberty attaching to associations and institutions with which the individual is concerned. This is not the familiar distinction between ' civil ' and ' political,' or even ' social,' liberty as it is ordinarily drawn ; for a liberty attaching to the individual *qua* individual may be political or economic in its content as well as civil. It is a distinction, not in the *content* of the liberty, but in its form of expression, between the liberty of personal freedom and the liberty of free and self-governing association.

It has often been pointed out that, if every individual is left absolutely free and unrestricted, the result, taken as a whole, is not liberty but anarchy. Nominally free, in such circumstances, the individual has really no freedom because he has no security or safeguard, and no certainty of the way in which other people will behave towards him. But it is no less true that, even if a community possesses a complete and all-pervading system of free and self-governing association, the individual is not necessarily any more free, because the associations may so trammel his liberty as to leave him no range for free choice or personal self-expression. In other words, ' free ' institutions do not necessarily carry with them personal liberty, any more than personal ' unrestrainedness ' can by itself secure real personal freedom. The two manifestations of liberty are complementary, and neither of them can be complete, or even real, without the other.

It will be noticed that in the last paragraph there was not an exact parallel between our two cases. I did not say that, whereas personal ' unrestrainedness ' could not guarantee personal freedom, neither could the unrestrained freedom of associations guarantee the real liberty of associations. In both cases, the end in view was the liberty of the individual ; for, in the last resort, the word ' liberty ' has no meaning except in reference to the individual. We may speak, if we will, of a ' free country ' or a ' free Church ' ; but in both cases we mean a freedom which belongs to the individuals who are members of the body or community concerned.

Here we are compelled to draw a further distinction. The idea of liberty directly applying to the individual *qua* individual is a simple idea, and does mean simply ' being let alone,' with only the qualification that this ' being let alone ' is an abstraction unless and until it is brought into relation to the other kind of liberty, and regarded as complementary with it. But the idea of social liberty, or liberty as attaching directly to associations, is a complex idea, and includes two distinguishable elements. It implies first the freedom of the association from external dictation *in respect of its manner of performing its function*, and it implies equally the internal self-government and democratic character of the association itself. Thus, when we speak of a ' free State,' we mean both a State which is not subject to any other State, and a State which is democratically governed. *Personal liberty* is thus simple and *external*; *social liberty* dual, and both *external* and *internal*.

This difference arises, of course, from the fact that, *qua* individual, the individual directly translates his will into deed, without the need for an intervening organisation, whereas the individual can only act socially through an association or intermediary, so that the need arises for a second type of social liberty, the equivalent of which is directly guaranteed to us as individuals by our possession of free will.[1]

Of *social liberty*, or the liberty of associations, it is not necessary to add much to what has already been said. The *internal* liberty of associations consists in their democratic character, and in the truly representative character of their forms of government and administration. Their external liberty consists in their freedom from interference from outside *in the performance of their functions*. The point which I have thus emphasised twice by the use of italics is of the first importance. The external liberty of an association consists not in its freedom from all interference from outside, but in its freedom in relation to its function. Such interference as is necessary to co-ordinate its function

[1] It will, of course, be seen that I am here refraining from entering into the oldest ethical controversy in the world. In such an ethical theory as that of Kant, personal freedom of course has its *internal* character of self-determination as well as the *external* character of ' unrestrainedness.'

with those of other associations is not a diminution of freedom, and interference arising from a departure by the association from its function is still less so ; for the association exists for the performance of its function and for nothing else, and, as soon as it steps outside its function, its rights lapse because it ceases to possess to its members a true representative relation.[1]

Personal liberty also is so simple an idea in itself as to need no detailed separate treatment. It is simply the freedom of the individual to express without external hindrance his ' personality '— his likes and dislikes, desires and aversions, hopes and fears, his sense of right and wrong, beauty and ugliness, and so on.

But to treat these two forms of liberty separately leads us nowhere. They acquire a real meaning only when they are brought into relation and when their complementary character is fully revealed. Until that is done they remain abstractions.

Let us remember above all that liberty as a whole has a meaning only in relation to the individual. Society and the community itself have no meaning apart from the individuals composing them, and to treat them as ' ends in themselves ' is to fall into an error which vitiates every conclusion based upon it. When, therefore, we seek to bring personal and social liberty into a complementary relation, what we are all really doing is to seek that relation between

[1] This statement must be taken in connexion with the remarks on ' perversion of function ' in Chapter III. ; for where perversion in one case causes perversion in another, the association may acquire a secondary ' counter-perversionary ' function which upholds its representative relation.

LIBERTY

them which will secure the greatest liberty for all
the individuals in a community, both severally and
in association. It is not a question of striking a
balance between the claims and counter-claims of
the individual and of Society, but of determining
what amount of organisation and what absence of
organisation will secure to the individual the greatest
liberty as the result of a blending of personal and
social liberties.

First of all, it is necessary to rid ourselves once
and for all of the notion that organisation is in itself
a good thing. It is very easy to fall into the notion
that growing complexity is a sign of progress, and
that the expanding organisation of Society is a sign
of the coming of the Co-operative Commonwealth.
A constantly growing measure of co-operation among
men is no doubt the greatest social need of our day ;
but co-operation has its unorganised as well as its
organised forms, and certainly the unorganised co-
operation of men, based on a sheer feeling of community, is not less valuable than organised co-operation, which may or may not have this feeling of
community behind it. It is easier to do most
things with organisation than without ; but organisation is to a great extent only the scaffolding
without which we should find the temple of human
co-operation too difficult to build.

To say this is not to decry organisation : it is only
to refrain from worshipping it. Organisation is a
marvellous instrument through which we every
day accomplish all manner of achievements which
would be inconceivable without it : but it is none
the less better to do a thing without organisation if

we can, or with the minimum of organisation that is necessary. For all organisation, as we have seen, necessarily carries with it an irreducible minimum of distortion of human purpose : it always comes down, to some extent, to letting other people do things for us instead of doing them ourselves, to allowing, in some measures, the wills of ' representatives ' to be substituted for our own wills. Thus, while it makes possible in one way a vast expansion of the field of self-expression that is open to the individual, it also in another way distorts that expression and makes it not completely the individual's own.

In complex modern communities there are so many things that must be organised that it becomes more than ever important to preserve from organisation that sphere in which it adds least to, and is apt to detract most from, our field of self-expression —the sphere of personal relationships and personal conduct. Legislation in recent times has tended more and more to encroach upon this sphere, not so much directly as by indirect roads, and especially owing to the operation of economic causes. Those measures of organisation and social coercion which trench upon the personal liberty of the individual or of the family are almost all directly traceable to economic causes, and fundamentally, to the existence of economic inequality in the community. They are the repercussions of the mal-distribution of property and income upon the personal lives of the poorer sections of the community. Given even an approximate economic equality, there would be no need for them.

LIBERTY

This is a sign of the manner in which bad organisation, or lack of free organisation of a particular social function, at once causes perversion in other spheres, not only by causing one association to usurp the function of another, but by causing organisation to take place, and compulsion to be applied, where personal liberty ought most to be preserved. The first necessity for concrete liberty for the individual lies in proper free functional organisation of those things which cannot be done without association. This alone makes it possible to leave untouched those spheres of human action which are spoiled by organisation.

This argument can be stated more particularly in another way. Economic equality is essential to personal freedom in the sphere of personal and family relations. But free, or democratic, functional organisation in the economic sphere is essential to the maintenance of economic equality. Therefore free economic organisation is essential to personal liberty in the sphere of personal relations.

But the individual will rightly refuse to be content with a personal liberty which is confined to the sphere of personal relations. Such liberty is vital to him ; but it is also vital to him to be personally free in his associative relations, that is, in relation to the associations of which he is a member, or which affect him by their operations. In relation to the associations of which he is a member, he will demand social freedom, that is, a right to a full share in their government and control. But this will not suffice for him. In addition to this social freedom which he and his fellows will claim to enjoy in relation

to the associations to which they belong, each of
them severally will claim personal liberty in the
sense of freedom from being tyrannised over even
by an association in whose decisions he has a
voice and vote. What safeguard can there be
for personal freedom in relation to associations,
that is, what safeguard against the tyranny of
majorities ?

It is folly to attempt, as some theorists do, to
answer this argument by a blank denial of the possibility of such tyranny. A majority can be just as
tyrannical as a minority. A decision does not
become *my* personal decision by the fact that it is
carried against my vote in an association of which
I am a member. There is no ' paradox ' of self-
government in this sense, no social miracle by which
my will can be transmuted into its direct opposite
by the operation of democracy. It is not my real
will to carry out every decision of a majority of an
association to which I happen to belong, however
silly or wrong I may believe it to be.

In most forms of social theory, this problem
assumes a false and misleading aspect by being
confined to my relations to one particular form of
association. The State is first assumed to be an
altogether superior kind of association or super-
association, quite different from all the other associations to which a man may belong. It is then
assumed that he stands in quite a different relation
to the State from his relation to any other association. And, whereas no one in his senses would
believe that it is my real will to carry out all the
decisions of my cricket club, without questioning,

men can be brought to think of the State so as to say :

> " Theirs not to reason why :
> Theirs but to do and die."

If our analysis of the nature of association and our account of the nature of the State as merely one form of association are correct, it is " theirs to reason why " either in relation to all associations or to none. We may be prepared to stretch more points in favour of accepting a decision of the State than of the cricket club, because we regard the maintenance of the State as more important ; but, if we reason at all, we must apply our reason to the decrees of State as well as to those of other associations. A difference of degree may remain ; but the difference in kind has disappeared.

According, therefore, to the social theory advanced in this book, a man owes not one absolute social loyalty and other subordinate loyalties which must always, in case of need, be overridden by it, but a number of relative and limited loyalties, of varying importance and intensity, but not essentially differing in kind. If this is so, and if the association to which we owe our ultimate loyalty is not externally determined for us by the character of the association itself, it follows that the choice of ultimate loyalty, in a case where loyalties conflict, necessarily resides in the individual himself.

It is true that the functional Society which we envisage includes in its structure forms of co-ordination and, in the last resort, coercion. Thus, in making his choice of loyalties, the individual cannot choose without incurring a risk of penalty, and does not escape altogether from the possibility of being coerced. That, however, is not the immediate point which I have in mind, though I shall be dealing with it before this chapter has grown much longer. The immediate point is that of the *moral* and not of the physical, or coercive, obligation upon the individual, and a great moral victory is won for individual liberty by the successful assertion of the individual's ultimate and unassailable moral right to choose for himself among conflicting social loyalties. Even if Society punishes him for choosing in a manner contrary to that prescribed by its co-ordinating organisation, it has no right to blame him or call him 'traitor' merely because his choice is contrary to the social precept. It is his business how he chooses, even if the consequences are still a sphere for social definition.[1]

Moral immunity, however, may seem to afford but cold comfort. What most people will want to know is how the individual would be practically situated if, in a case of conflict of loyalties, his decision ran counter to that of the co-ordinating organisation of Society. I believe that the position of the individual would be greatly more favourable than it is, or can be, under State Sovereignty or any unitary form of Sovereignty, or, in other words, than it can be under any system in which the supreme social authority is vested in a single body or association. In this case at least, there is 'safety in numbers,' and hope for the individual in the balance

---

[1] Definition before the event, of course. The objection to the retrospective creation of offences holds good all the more if this view is accepted.

of functional associations in Society. Unitary theories of Sovereignty, or the existence in fact of Societies in which one association is supreme, are invitations to tyranny, because they are based upon the inclusion of all the individuals in a single organisation. If the Sovereign State is the representative of everybody, the individual is manifestly less than the Sovereign State which claims, by virtue of its superiority, a right to do with and to him what it pleases—in the interests of all or the whole, *bien entendu.*

But, under a functional system, each individual is a member of many associations, and each has upon him only a limited claim—limited by its social function. The position of the individual as the source and sustaining spirit of every association is therefore clear, and the associations show plainly as only partial expressions and extensions of the will of the individual. They have thus no superiority over him, and their claim is limited to what he surrenders to them for the performance of their functions.

Will not a Society based upon these principles be likely to be far less prone to tyranny than any other sort of Society? It must be remembered that the functional character of all its associations will make them far more truly representative, and therefore far more likely to sustain the will to liberty among their members. The best guarantee of personal liberty that can exist is in the existence, in each form of association, of an alert democracy, keenly critical of every attempt of the elected person and the official to pass beyond his representative function. In a Society made up of a multiplicity of such associations, there would be less reason than in any other that is practically possible for the emergence of tyranny and the submergence of personal liberty beneath the weight of social organisation. The safeguards are not absolute ; but they are as good as we can hope for at present. The functional organisation of Society contains in itself the guarantee of the recognition of the fact that Society is based upon the individuals, exists in and for the individuals, and can never transcend the wills of the individuals who compose it.

CHAPTER XIII

THE ATROPHY OF INSTITUTIONS

THERE is always a danger attendant upon theoretical studies of presenting as static and at rest what is essentially dynamic and in motion. This risk is peculiarly great in the domain of social theory ; for it is difficult to refrain from hardening universal principles, or principles which at least seem to be universal, into precepts, and from claiming the same universality for the precept as for the principle. Utopias are almost always unsatisfactory, because they almost always depict a community from which factors of vital change and development have been eliminated.

It is therefore of the first importance that we should remember that neither the human wills which make Societies and communities, nor the material circumstances upon which these wills work, have any but a relative degree of permanence. Material circumstances alter, and their alteration compels men to adopt new methods of living and working together. And on the other hand, men's desires and aspirations change, and they seek different methods of co-operation from time to time and from place to place, even if the material conditions remain the same.

AN INTRODUCTION TO SOCIAL THEORY

There is, as we have seen, a strong element of artifice about all forms of social organisation. Associations are designed, more or less deliberately, for the fulfilment of certain purposes. Even customs, which seem the most unconscious things, are for the most part only purposes become ' mechanical ' by force of long habit. If will is the basis of Society, habit is certainly the cement which holds its structure together.

This ' force of habit,' which is so powerful a factor in the working of Societies, as well as in the unorganised social life of communities, has two contrasted aspects. It helps men to live together in Societies and communities without pushing their constant disagreements to the point of open conflict ; for men will tolerate calmly an evil (in their eyes) to which they are accustomed, whereas they would fiercely resent and resist its introduction. The influence of habit, thus checking the desire for re-organisation and change, causes changes for the most part to take place gradually without any profound disturbance of the life of the community, or of the structure of the Society within it.

This is the good side of habit, without which the stable existence of Society, and even of the community itself, would be difficult, if not impossible. But habit has another side, and here its operations are by no means an unmixed blessing. It not only offers resistance to changes which would imperil the stability of Society, but often to changes which are necessary for its preservation and development. It not only prevents the primitive destruction of associations or institutions or customs which incur a temporary unpopularity, but helps to preserve associations or institutions or customs which have lost all social utility, or which are actively retarding the processes of social development.

Even an individual, when he 'changes his mind,' by casting off an old belief, or prejudice, or fruit of bad reasoning, does not usually do so by a quite sudden and simple act of conversion. He ordinarily passes through a period of doubt, and, if the belief which is being discarded has with it a strong force of custom or habit, he will often continue to act on the old belief until the long process of conversion is absolutely complete, and even after it is complete when his will is not vigilant to prevent him from doing so. Far more is this the case with social changes. Associations, institutions and customs continue apparently in full force, not only while the faith of men in their social utility is passing away, but even long after it has passed away. So strong is the social force of habit, not only upon the individual, but still more upon crowds, organised groups and communities.

It is therefore a phenomenon found in almost every community at almost every stage of its development that, side by side with fully-grown associations, institutions and customs, and with such as are beginning to grow and to achieve recognition, there exist other associations, institutions and customs which have lost their savour and social utility, or, to use a convenient phrase, have become *atrophied*. Moreover, it will often be found that these atrophied social phenomena occupy, at any rate conventionally, the highest place in social honour, and appear on the surface as integral parts of the structure of Society and necessary bonds of community.

Samuel Butler, who has stated far better than anyone else the social force and character of habit and 'unconscious memory,' made, in his *Erewhon* novels, the best existing study of this phenomenon of atrophy. The 'Musical Banks' of Erewhon, whatever their application to our own Society, form the best possible example of an atrophied institution, and the worship of the goddess ' Ydgrun '—more familiarly known in this country as Mrs. Grundy—expresses the power of habit over us which causes such survivals. There are, no doubt, extreme cases ; but anyone can think of instances in which the social status of a firmly and long-established institution is out of all proportion to its surviving social utility.

This phenomenon of survival of the 'shell' when the function has passed from it occurs principally in the case of those social forms which we decided to call 'institutions.' [1] It will be remembered that we there defined an *institution* as ' an idea which is manifested concretely in some aspect of social conduct, and which forms a part of the underlying assumptions of communal life.' We also said that it may be manifested either ' in men's personal conduct or relationships or through organised groups or associations.'

An institution, then, may be embodied in an association ; but neither are all institutions embodied in associations, nor do all associations embody

[1] See Chapter II., pp. 41 ff.

institutions. An institution is a social form, whether it be embodied in an association, or a custom or something else, which has behind it a strong 'force of habit' based upon a historic importance of function. There are thus two elements which go to the conferring of institutional status. *An idea* only acquires the status of an institution by performing over a considerable period of time an essential social function, and thus becoming important to men's habits as well as to their reasons; but, this status once acquired, habit will usually outlast reason, and maintain the institution in being and in enjoyment of status after its function has ceased to exist or be socially important.

I have said that an association may embody, or enjoy the status of, an institution, and in the second chapter I instanced States and Churches as examples of this. As we saw in Chapter II., an association is not an institution, but it may become the embodiment or social expression of an institution. Strictly speaking, it is not 'the State' that is an institution, but social order, of which the State is regarded, on the score of certain past services, as the embodiment—not 'the Church,' but the Spirit of God on earth, which the Church with its apostolic tradition is regarded as expressing. An institution is always at bottom an idea, a belief or a commandment, and never an actual thing. It attaches itself to things, but it is not identical with things.

This difference has to be brought out in order to explain fully how we manage at all to rid ourselves of atrophied institutions, or, as we should now say, atrophied expressions of institutions. Where the idea or belief itself, that is to say the institution itself becomes atrophied, the force of habit finally dies out, and the institution passes away, perhaps long after the usefulness has been outlived. But where the idea or belief remains vital, but the association or law or custom in which it is embodied ceases, under altered conditions, truly to express it, there, failing the adaptation of the association, law or custom, the idea which is the real 'soul' of the institution transfers itself to some other law or custom, and the old 'body' of the institution decays and finally disappears. In this case, too, there is probably a long period during which, though the soul has departed from it, the body of the institution continues apparently to flourish, and retains its social status to all outward seeming unimpaired.[1]

In our treatment of associations, we dwelt on the fact that often, in the history of Societies, the same function passes at different periods from one association to another. Thus, industry passed from the Mediæval Guilds to the capitalist employer, and is now passing, at least in part, into the control of the Trade Unions. But some Mediæval Guilds still linger on in the atrophied form of Livery Companies, and, when Capitalism has ceased to exist, certainly if there is no violent revolution, and probably even if there is, atrophied

---

[1] Foreign observers often mistake such atrophied bodies of institutions for the real soul of a people. The pre-revolutionary legend of Russia, as told for example by Mr. Stephen Graham, furnishes a good example.

survivals of capitalist association will continue in existence.

In the sphere of social organisation, it is profoundly true that

> ' Each age is a dream that is dying,
> And one that is coming to birth.'

For the associations, customs, laws and conventions among which we live are a queer mixture of obsolete and obsolescent survivals from the past, with other social forms ' in the prime of life,' and yet others which are only beginning to assume the true social shape of their maturity. The social prophet is not he who builds Utopias out of his own imagination, but he who can see in these rising associations, in these laws which are ' precedents,' and in these forming habits the signs of the future, and can rightly say whither they are tending or what social functions they can be made to serve. The soundest part of the Marxian philosophy is that which inculcates the lesson that the structure of a new social order must be built up within the old while it is still in being, and that the face of Society can only be changed when new associations and ways of life have been created within the fabric of the old in readiness to take its place.

It is true that this doctrine appears in Marxism coupled with the deadening determinism which vitiates the whole system. The appearance of the new forms within the old is made to appear as something inevitable, and not as the product of will and effort. Even as we followed Samuel Butler in applying to social theory his doctrine of habit, we may follow him here in applying his doctrine of evolution. Let us be, as he would have said, Lamarckians rather than Darwinians in our theory of social development. We need not deny or minimise the vast influence of material conditions in causing social changes and directing the course of social development ; but we can still believe that the creation of new social forms for old, and still more the right direction and utilisation of those new social forms which arise out of changing material conditions, is a matter which human wills can influence and which indeed depend essentially upon men's active will to take advantage of their opportunities.

CHAPTER XIV

CONCLUSION

THE foregoing chapters embody an attempt to state, in the smallest possible compass, the essential principles of social organisation. Their primary concern has been not with the actual associations which exist in the community, nor with any attempt at classifying the various forms of association, but with the moral and psychological problems underlying social organisation in its actual and possible forms among men and in communities like our own. This limitation is necessary, because it may be that there are peoples and communities so different from our own that the generalisations which we make for ourselves out of our own experience simply do not apply to them, or apply only with changes so fundamental as to be incalculable by us. In Western Europe, the conditions, psychological and material, which underlie social organisation are homogeneous enough to admit of generalisations that possess a real content. But I should hesitate to apply even to Russia generalisations based on West European study and experience, and still less should I venture to apply them to the civilisations of the East. It must be enough for us if we can make a social theory which will explain our own communities, and help us to bring them, in their structure and functioning, into a more real harmony with the wills of the men and women of whom they are composed.

There are many persons, considering themselves as practically-minded, who scorn altogether the sort of social theory with which this book is concerned. In their eyes, social and political practice is a mass of expedients, devised to overcome particular difficulties, and not derivable from any philosophic theory of Society. You can, they hold, usefully classify and arrange for future reference these various expedients ; you can make lists of the forms of social organisation, and study, by the method of comparison, the actual expedients employed in various communities. But they hold that it is useless to attempt, from the study of these expedients, to discover universal principles, or to pretend to find in them the working of certain universal ideas of human association.

That the ac'ual structure of existing Societies is to a great extent made up of political and social expedients devised, with no theoretic *arrière-pensée*, to meet particular problems, I most fully agree ; but it has been part of my purpose to show that these expedients, both in their successes and still more in their failures, clearly reveal the working of the universal principles upon which the main stress has been laid. The clash between the actual structure of present-day communities and the general principles which govern success in social

CONCLUSION

organisation is manifest in every aspect of the communal life to-day—not only in that organised part of it which we have called Society, but in its reaction upon the unorganised parts of the lives of the men and women who are the members of the community. Society to-day is, indeed, a "big, booming, buzzing confusion," and it will continue to be impossible to clear this confusion away until we realise that its causes lie in our ignoration of the most essential conditions of successful association—the principles of democratic functional organisation and democratic representation according to function.

While we recognise, however, that much of the *malaise* of communities to-day arises from the failure of their leaders to grasp and apply these fundamental principles, it is equally essential to understand that these principles themselves are not the inventions of the theorist or social philosopher, but are, however imperfectly, at work everywhere around us in Society. Everywhere men's striving to find expression for their social purposes leads them to base their action upon these principles, and everywhere they find themselves thwarted by actual forms of organisation which run directly counter to them, either because of the atrophy of a once useful form or because some vested interest has interfered so as to cause a perversion or opposition of function among essential forms of association. Society is everywhere the scene of conflict between the spontaneous outbursts of the principle of functional democracy and the resistance of established associations and institutions which are

203

either based upon, or have come to stand for, a perversion of social function.

In these circumstances, it is natural that the true principles of social organisation usually find their purest expression in the associations of revolt. There is a tendency, in some degree inevitable, of things established and powerful to deteriorate and suffer perversion, and, in any Society, the recall to sanity will largely come from those spontaneous groupings which form themselves in opposition to the groups in power. This tendency would exist even in the most perfectly organised community ; but it is greatly intensified in the communities of to-day by the almost complete absence of any functional principle in the groups which at present hold the recognised forms of social power. The promise of the Society of to-morrow is in the revolts of to-day.

I have tried to make as clear as possible throughout this book that human Society is neither a mechanism nor an organism. It is not a machine which we can invent and put together at will in the measure of our collective capacity ; and still less is it a thing that grows without being made by our wills. We cannot describe its processes of growth and change in terms of any other body of knowledge, natural or unnatural. It has a method and processes of its own. Thus, a group of men living together in some particular relation within a community needs something. There may be a dozen different ways in which the need can be met. Perhaps no one devises a way of meeting it, and in that case the need goes unsatisfied. Perhaps,

CONCLUSION

on the other hand, someone, or the group as a whole, finds, or stumbles upon, a way either of creating some new organisation to supply the need, or of adapting an existing organisation to deal with it. More or less successfully, the necessary steps are taken, and a new social development is inaugurated. This development would not take place without the need being more or less clearly present—that is the material or environmental basis of social organisation. But neither would the development take place unless human wills devised a way of meeting the need—that is its human or psychological basis.

This, however, is only the first stage in the development. The new, or re-created, organisation arises to meet a need ; but it not only more or less perfectly meets the need, but also exerts an influence on the other organisations which exist side by side with it in the community. It has therefore next to find its proper place in the general structure of Society and in the community as a whole. As an actual organisation, it presents itself as a fact of which Society has to take account. Here, again, the factor of human will comes into play. There may be a dozen different ways, of varying merit, of assigning to the new organisation its place and recognition in Society. Perhaps none of these ways, or a bad way, is adopted. In that case, the new organisation acts as a disruptive force in Society, and may, if it is strong enough, end by tearing the social structure asunder, and compelling a fundamental reconstruction. Or, on the other hand, it may be itself destroyed, even if it is performing a useful function in Society. Perhaps, however, a reasonable way is found of fitting the new organisation into the social structure. In that case, the new organisation enters into the structure of Society, and in doing so both modifies Society as a whole and is itself modified. These are the normal and peculiar processes of social development.

I am labouring this point in order to make it clear that important social changes are usually inaugurated in the parts and not in the whole of Society, and often nearer to its circumference than to its centre. It is usually difficult, and often impossible, to foresee in the early stages of such a process as I have described the nature or extent of the social change that is really beginning. The best social prophet and the best constructive states-man are those who have most the power of divining, among the many new movements and associations which are constantly arising and among the old ones which are constantly undergoing modification to suit new needs, those particular organisations which are most likely to effect large changes in the whole structure of Society.

This may seem a truism ; but it has a moral which is not so generally recognised. " Keep your eye on the new movements and organisations, and always estimate them in accordance less with what they actually are than with what they seem capable of becoming " is the first maxim of social wisdom. Big social changes are seldom, if ever, created or at least maintained, unless the impetus to change has behind it the force of an organised

CONCLUSION

group or association based on a vital common need. In the welter of revolution, the power to build a new order will belong to those who have behind them the most coherent form of social organisation, the form best fitted among those available to replace the old order and provide for the effective fulfilment of vital social functions. It is the possession by the working-class movements of such strong and purposeful forms of organisation as Trade Unionism and Co-operation that makes their inheritance of the task of reconstructing Society almost certain.

No doubt, it will be said that this conviction of the coming of a new order, called into being largely as a result of the emergence of the new forms of social power which these working-class movements represent, has coloured much of the writing contained in this book. Of course it has done so. It is the business of the theorist to interpret in terms of ideas the actual forces and tendencies by which he is surrounded. Anyone with the smallest degree of social vision can see that the existing structure of Society is doomed either to ignominious collapse or to radical transformation. Anyone ought to be able to see that the social theories based upon this structure are bound to share its fate. Theory which is content merely to interpret the established order will inevitably misinterpret; for the truth about the established order is only visible when that order is confronted with its successor growing up within itself. Theory ought to get ahead of actual development; for the chief value of theory lies in helping men to act more intelligently in the present by giving them a power to grasp the principles which must go to make the future. These principles— any social principles—are, of course, only true upon certain assumptions ; and I have not hesitated to make certain assumptions the basis on which the whole theory of this book is built. What are these assumptions ?

I assume that the object of social organisation is not merely material efficiency, but also essentially the fullest self-expression of all the members. I assume that self-expression involves self-govern- ment, and that we ought to aim not merely at giving people votes, but at calling forth their full participation in the common direction of the affairs of the community.

If anyone questions these assumptions, there is no way of proving them either true or untrue. If it is contended that men only ask for peace and quietness, and do not want to govern themselves, I answer in the first place that this is not true, and, secondly, that, if it were true, we ought not to acquiesce in such a state of affairs, but to alter it as speedily as possible. In short, it has been assumed throughout this book that human beings have wills, and that they have a right and duty to use those wills to their full capacity in the direction of Society. These, I think, are my only assumptions. For the rest, the arguments used to prove each point may be sound or they may be unsound. No doubt they are mixed ; but my object has been not to achieve finality or write a definitive book, but to set others to work upon

CONCLUSION

problems which I have only raised. The time for a new and definitive social theory is not yet ; but it is high time for our generation to set about laying the foundations of a theory more responsive to modern development than that which at present holds sway. Orthodox social theory is bankrupt : it neither corresponds to the facts of to-day, nor affords any help in interpreting the tendencies which are shaping a new social order within the old. There are already, in the writings of such men as Maitland, Figgis, and the Guild Socialists, some of the elements necessary to a new theory ; and my main object has been to express what seem to me the essential principles of this theory, certainly not in a final, but, I hope, in an intelligible form, in order that, even if they are not accepted, they may at least be criticised and discussed.

BIBLIOGRAPHICAL NOTES

THERE is, of course, an immense literature dealing with social and political theory in its various aspects and from different points of view. These notes are not intended to do more than indicate a few of the books which I have found most useful, by way either of attraction or of repulsion, in forming my own view. The list could be indefinitely prolonged.

(A.) GENERAL

MACIVER, R. M.—*Community, a Sociological Study.* (Macmillan.)
    [This is by far the best general book I know. It is especially useful on the nature of community and for the study of associations.]

ROUSSEAU, J. J.—*Social Contract and Discourses*, edited and translated by G. D. H. Cole. (Dent.)
    [Rousseau's *Social Contract* remains by far the greatest and most stimulating study of the basis of social obligation.]

BARKER, E.—*Political Thought from Herbert Spencer to the Present Day.* (Williams & Norgate.)
    [A useful introductory study.]

BURNS, C. DELISLE.—*Political Ideals.* (Oxford University Press.)
    [A short study of the historical development of political ideals.]

BIBLIOGRAPHY

(*B.*) SPECIAL

CHAPTER I

WALLAS, GRAHAM.—*Human Nature in Politics.* (Constable.)
—— *The Great Society.* (Macmillan.)
LIPPMANN, WALTER.—*A Preface to Politics.* (Mitchell Kennerley.)
BROWN, W. JETHRO.—*The Principles underlying Modern Legislation.* (Murray.)
RITCHIE, D. G.—*Natural Rights.* (G. Allen & Unwin).
—— *Darwinism and Politics.* (G. Allen & Unwin.)
BOSANQUET, BERNARD.—*The Philosophical Theory of the States.* (Macmillan.)
ANSON, SIR W. R.—*The Law and Custom of the Constitution.* (Oxford University Press.)
DICEY, A. V.—*The Law of the Constitution.* (Macmillan.)
POLLOCK, SIR F.—*History of the Science of Politics.* (Macmillan.)
JENKS, EDWARD.—*The State and the Nation.* (Dent.)
BAGEHOT, WALTER.—*Physics and Politics.* (Kegan Paul.)
—— *The English Constitution.* (Nelson.)
MACDOUGALL, WILLIAM.—*Social Psychology.* (Methuen.)
MACDONALD, J. R.—*Socialism and Society.* (Independent Labour Party.)

CHAPTER II

MACIVER.—*Op. cit.*

CHAPTER III

PLATO.—*Republic,* translated by A. D. Lindsay. (Dent.)
BARKER, E.—*The Political Thought of Plato and Aristotle.* (Methuen.)
DE MAEZTU, RAMIRO.—*Authority, Liberty and Function.* (G. Allen & Unwin.)

AN INTRODUCTION TO SOCIAL THEORY

HOBSON, S. G., and ORAGE, A. R.—*National Guilds*. (Bell.)
COLE, G. D. H.—*Self-Government in Industry*. (Bell.)
—— *Labour in the Commonwealth*. (Headley.)

CHAPTER IV

MACIVER.—*Op. cit.*
GIERKE, O.—*Political Theories of the Middle Ages*, edited with an Introduction by F. W. Maitland. (Cambridge University Press.)

CHAPTER V AND CHAPTER VIII

LASKI, H. J.—*Studies in the Problem of Sovereignty*. (Oxford University Press.)
—— *Authority in the Modern State*. (Oxford University Press.)
BOSANQUET, B.—*Op. cit.*
HOBHOUSE, L. T.—*The Metaphysical Theory of the State*. (G. Allen & Unwin.)
PAUL, WILLIAM.—*The State : its Origin and Function*. (Socialist Labour Press.)
COLE, G. D. H.—*Op. cit.*
BROWN, W. JETHRO.—*The Austinian Theory of Law*. (John Murray.)

CHAPTERS VI-VII

ROUSSEAU.—*Op. cit.*
MICHELS, R.—*Democracy and the Organisation of Political Parties*.
BELLOC, HILAIRE, and CHESTERTON, CECIL.—*The Party System*. (Swift.)
MILL, J. S.—*Representative Government*.

CHAPTER IX

MARX, KARL.—*Capital*. 3 volumes.
—— and ENGELS, F.—*The Communist Manifesto*.

BIBLIOGRAPHY

PAUL, WILLIAM.—*Op. cit.*
HOBSON and ORAGE.—*Op. cit.*
COLE.—*Op. cit.*

CHAPTER X

FAWCETT, C. B.—*The Natural Divisions of England.* (Royal Geographical Society.)
—— *The Provinces of England.* (Williams & Norgate.)
BRUN, CHARLES.—*Le Régionalisme.*

CHAPTER XI

FIGGIS, J. N.—*Churches in the Modern State.* (Longmans.)
ROBERTS, R.—*The Church in the Commonwealth.* (Headley.)
MARSON, C. L.—*God's Co-operative Society.* (Longmans.)
Report of the Archbishops' Committee on Church and State.

CHAPTER XII

RUSSELL, BERTRAND.—*Roads to Freedom.* (G. Allen & Unwin.)
—— *Principles of Social Reconstruction.* (G. Allen & Unwin.)
MILL, J. S.—*Liberty.*
CECIL, LORD HUGH.—*Liberty and Authority.* (Edward Arnold.)

CHAPTER XIII

BUTLER, SAMUEL.—*Erewhon.* (Fifield.)
—— *Life and Habit.* (Fifield.)
WARD, JAMES.—*Heredity and Memory.* (Cambridge University Press.)

INDEX

Action, relation to organisation, 33
Ad hoc organisation, 99 f., 168
Administration, 113, 162. *See also* Government
— regional, 166
A. E., 35
Air Force, 141
Amalgamation, 58
American social theory, 19
Analogies, use of, 14
Anarchy, 181
Anthropology, 18
Areas, 158 ff.
Army, 42, 141, 142
Associations, 5, 7, 9, 11, 14, 17, 25, 26, 30, 35-6, 53, Chap IV., 104, 125, 207
— administrative, 72, 74
— appetitive, 68-9, 134 f.
— coercion in, 128
— definition of, 32 ff., 37
— development of, 56
— diseases of, 18
—' essential,' 65 ff., 74, 75 ff., 134 f.
— forms of, Chap. IV.
— government of, 104 ff., 117 ff.
— motives of, 77 ff.
— philanthropic, 71
— political, 67, 134. *See also* State and Local Government
— propagandist, 73-4
— provident, 70
— relation to institutions, 196 ff.
— religious, 69-70. *See also* Churches
— rules of, 40

Associations, sociable, 71
— theoretical, 71-72
— vocational, 68, 72, 97, 134 f., 136. *See also* Trade Unions and Employers' Associations
Assumptions, social, 208
Atrophy, social, 38, 39, 43 ff., 75, Chap. XIII., 203
Austinian theory of law, 5, 212
Australia, 164

Balance of Powers, 124-5
Belloc, Hilaire, 122, 151, 152, 212
'Black Lists,' 129
Bolshevism, 10, 61
Bosanquet, Bernard, 22, 93, 211
British Empire, 164
Burke, Edmund, 22
Butler, Samuel, 45 196, 199, 213

Cabinet system, the, 108, 122
Canada, 164
Capitalism, 42, 147 ff., 198
Caste, 42
Catholicism, Roman, 89, 172
Charity organisation, 70
Chesterton, Cecil, 122, 212
Chesterton, G. K., 160
Children, 130
Church and State, 138, 172, 177
— of England, 172
Churches, 9, 10, 18, 22, 38, 42, 61, 70, 73, 76, 101, 129, Chap. XI.
— as institutions, 197

215

AN INTRODUCTION TO SOCIAL THEORY

INDEX

INDEX

PRINTED BY MORRISON AND GIBB LIMITED, EDINBURGH

For Product Safety Concerns and Information please contact our EU
representative GPSR@taylorandfrancis.com Taylor & Francis Verlag GmbH,
Kaufingerstraße 24, 80331 München, Germany

Printed and bound by CPI Group (UK) Ltd, Croydon, CR0 4YY
08/05/2025
01864391-0001